SEMINAR STUDIES IN HISTORY
General Editor: Roger Lockyer

The Third Republic from 1870 to 1914

Robert Gildea

LONGMAN
London and New York

Longman Group UK Limited,
Longman House, Burnt Mill, Harlow,
Essex CM20 2JE, England
and Associated Companies throughout the world.

Published in the United States of America
by Longman Inc., New York.

©Longman Group UK Limited 1988

First published 1988

Set in 10/11 point Baskerville (Linotron)
Produced by Longman Group (FE) Limited
Printed in Hong Kong

ISBN 0 582 35556 7

British Library Cataloguing in Publication Data
Gildea, Robert
 The Third Republic from 1870–1914. —
 (Seminar studies in history).
 1. France — History — Third Republic,
 1870–1940   2. France — Politics and
 government — 1870–1940
 I. Title   II. Series
 944.081   DC340

  ISBN 0-582-35556-7

Library of Congress Cataloging in Publication Data
Gildea, Robert.
  The Third Republic from 1870–1914 / Robert Gildea.
    p.   cm. — (Seminar studies in history)
  Bibliography: p.
  Includes index.
  ISBN 0-582-35556-7 : £3.25
  1. France — History — Third Republic, 1870–1940.   2. France —
Politics and government — 1870–1940.   I. Title.   II. Series.
DC335.G55 1988
944.081 — dc19   87-33551
                                                     CIP

Contents

Contents

Seminar Studies in History
Founding Editor: Patrick Richardson

Introduction

The Seminar Studies series was conceived by Patrick Richardson, whose experience of teaching history persuaded him of the need for something more substantial than a textbook chapter but less formidable than the specialised full-length academic work. He was also convinced that such studies, although limited in length, should provide an up-to-date authoritative introduction to the topic under discussion as well as a selection of relevant documents and a comprehensive bibliography.

Patrick Richardson died in 1979, but by that time the Seminar Studies series was firmly established, and it continues to fulfil the role he intended for it. This book, like others in the series, is therefore a living tribute to a gifted and original teacher.

Note on the System of References:
A bold number in round brackets (**5**) in the text refers the reader to the corresponding entry in the Bibliography section at the end of the book. A bold number in square brackets, preceded by 'doc.' [**doc. 6**] refers the reader to the corresponding item in the section of Documents, which follows the main text.

ROGER LOCKYER
General Editor

Acknowledgements

We are grateful to the following for permission to reproduce copyright material:

Editions Gallimard for an extract from pp. 44–6 *La France Radicale* by Jean-Thomas Nordmann © Editions Gallimard et Julliard 1977; Hachette for an extract from pp. 104–7 *L'Antimilitarisme Français* by Jean Rabaut.

Cover: Dreyfus's sword being broken. Photo: Roget-Viollet, Paris.

Part One: The Background

1 Which Republic?

The Third Republic happened almost by accident, but it was the most successful of all French republics, lasting from 1870 until 1940. The first two French republics had existed respectively for twelve and four years, each of them terminated when a Bonaparte assumed the imperial crown. The Third Republic was given its chance by the defeat of the Second Empire at the hands of Prussia, and would not have emerged so quickly, if at all, without that defeat. There was nothing 'inevitable' about it; indeed the pattern of French history was for monarchy to be displaced by republic, republic by empire and empire by monarchy. It was something of an oddity in the society of nations: France was the only major power in Europe after 1870 that was a republic. But unlike the First Republic of 1792–1804, the Third Republic did not have to fight for survival against a coalition of European monarchies. It lived in peace with its neighbours for two generations until 1914, and emerged victorious from the First World War in 1918, before it succumbed to the forces of the Third Reich in 1940 (**1–5**).

Although the Third Republic was born of military defeat, it is quite legitimate to speak of a republican tradition in France. Or more accurately of strands of a republican tradition, for not all republicans of 1870–1 were in the same vein. One strand was dictatorial and patriotic. These republicans were convinced of the absolute necessity of continuing the war against Prussia after the defeat of the Second Empire in order to preserve the Republic itself. The second element were liberals who thought that the Republic offered the best opportunity to safeguard parliamentary institutions which had been flouted by the Empire. They wanted to make peace with the Prussians as soon as possible, in order to prevent power from falling into the hands of a third group of republicans. These were the insurrectionaries. They were inspired by the Paris Commune of 1792, which had been thrown up by the *sans-culottes* in the teeth of invasion by Prussia and Austria and aristocratic treachery, and which saved France and founded the

First Republic. In similar circumstances they demanded the same desperate measures. Each group of republicans was epitomised by a single personality: the first by Gambetta, the second by Thiers, the third by Blanqui.

Léon Gambetta was a southerner, the son of a grocer, a lawyer, tribune of the people and fierce opponent of the Second Empire. Under the Empire, for the sake of prudence, he and his associates called themselves 'democrats' or 'radicals' rather than republicans. He was a champion of universal suffrage, as the vehicle of popular sovereignty. He supported parliamentary institutions, but was prepared to accept a mandate from the electors of Belleville, a suburb of Paris, in 1869, to press for such far-reaching democratic measures as the election of mayors, who were at that time appointed by the government. Gambetta was a republican, but opposed to revolution. He held to legality, took hope from the performance of the republicans in the elections of 1869, when they increased their representation in the Legislative Body from 35 to 87 seats, and he set about organising them into a viable force [**doc. 1a**]. This legality was something of a handicap, for universal suffrage, which had been established in 1848 and abrogated in 1850, had then been restored by Louis-Napoleon in 1851, and the source of greatest opposition – a lack of liberty – was remedied by the grant of a liberal constitution in 1870. When this was massively ratified by plebiscite, Gambetta had to confess that the Empire was stronger than ever; and that was only four months before it crumbled at Sedan.

A Republic was declared on 4 September 1870, and a Government of National Defence was set up to continue the war against the Prussians. The whole of northern France was occupied, Paris was cut off on 19 September, and in provincial towns such as Lyon and Marseille republican groups seized power and set up regional federations of republican strongholds in order to carry on the struggle as best they could (**6**). Gambetta emerged as the key figure in the Government of National Defence. As Minister for War, he was determined to win at any cost. This meant reinforcing the depleted regular army by raising an auxiliary citizen army which would fight alongside it (**7**). As Minister of the Interior, he tried to bring the provinces under his direct control by the appointment of republican prefects he could trust. Pressure was growing for the calling of a National Assembly to draw up a new constitution. Gambetta resisted this, fearing that such an assembly would be dominated by Bonapartists and royalists rather than republicans. A republican dictatorship was necessary in his eyes to preserve the Republic itself (**8**).

Not all the members of the Government of National Defence agreed with Gambetta. Foremost amongst these was Adolphe Thiers, an opposition journalist under the Restoration and many times minister under the July Monarchy. He was a liberal and parliamentarian, who detested the authoritarian Empire but disliked universal suffrage equally, and had supported the disenfranchisement of three million of the 'vile multitude' in 1850. Unlike Gambetta, he wanted to conclude an armistice as soon as possible with Prussia, and to hold elections for a National Assembly which would ratify peace terms. Thiers had his way. An armistice was signed in January 1871, and the following month elections were held. The electorate's priorities were peace and liberty. At the polls it rejected Bonapartists and Gambettist republicans as (in different ways) warmongering and dictatorial, and returned a stream of royalists, including two Orleanist princes. Although the National Assembly was royalist, there was no immediate danger of a royalist restoration. Royalist leaders were not keen to witness a third restoration at the hands of foreigners that century. And royalist deputies were anxious in the first instance to reassert the supremacy of parliament over the executive power. Nevertheless, in the crisis faced by France, executive power had to be delegated by the Assembly. Thiers, who had been elected in twenty-seven departments (elections were on a system of departmental proportional representation and candidates could stand in more than one department) was the obvious choice. Caught between a royalist Assembly and a Republic existing in fact, Thiers, by nature a trimmer, was reluctant to jump. But persuaded by republican leaders, he agreed to take the title 'Chief of the Executive Power of the French Republic'. This made possible the adherence to the Republic of practical men who were by inclination supporters of parliamentary monarchy (**9**).

Paris, meanwhile, which had been under Prussian siege since September 1870, was seething with revolutionaries who had no confidence either in the Government of National Defence or in the National Assembly. First there were Blanquists – comrades of Auguste Blanqui, an exponent of armed insurrection since 1830 and himself currently in prison. Next there were the Jacobins around Charles Delescluze who, unlike Gambetta, was a veteran of 1848 and was prepared to use revolutionary means in order to obtain a government fully accountable to the people. Finally there

3

were the adherents of the First Workers' International, grouped in sections and trade unions, numbering between 20,000 and 30,000 workers. The revolutionaries demanded direct democracy, or the retention of power in the hands of the people, not their elected representatives. The instruments of their power were: first vigilance committees in each of the twenty *arrondissements* of Paris, to keep often moderate mayors in revolutionary step [**doc. lb**]; second the National Guard, which had been banned under the Empire but was expanded by Gambetta to defend Paris, and had swollen to about 360,000; and third revolutionary clubs, the foci of heated political debate. The goal of the revolutionaries was the establishment of a central revolutionary organ to save Paris and the Republic. The enemy were both the Prussians who paraded insolently on the Champs Elysées in Paris by permission of Thiers on 1 March and those Frenchmen who believed that social order was more important than victory, and that the peace agreed by the National Assembly would have to be imposed on Paris by disarming the National Guard (**10**).

On 18 March 1871 regular troops were sent into Paris to seize the cannon held by the National Guard. But they were too few and unreliable, and many fraternised with the National Guard and the working-class populations of the suburbs who rose in their support. The central committee of the National Guard battalions, formed on 15 March, became a provisional revolutionary government in Paris as the executive power withdrew in disarray to Versailles. On 26 March a Commune to represent the whole of Paris (for the first time since the 1790s) was elected. It was dominated by National Guard militants, Blanquists, Jacobins, Internationalists and other socialists. For weeks the troops of the Commune and those of the government at Versailles were locked in combat, with the execution of hostages on both sides. But once the peace with newly-united Germany was signed at Frankfurt, the balance of forces shifted to Thiers, as Bismarck allowed 60,000 French prisoners of war to pass through German lines and attack Paris. In the brutal suppression of the *Semaine Sanglante* (Bloody Week) 25,000 Parisians were massacred. Of the 40,000 arrested, 10,000 were convicted, 5,000 sent to the penal colony of New Caledonia in the Pacific, 93 condemned to death and 23 executed. The Republic of Monsieur Thiers triumphed over the workers' Republic of the Commune, but the memory and mythology of the Commune would continue to define working-class culture and consciousness and perpetuate an irrational fear of class war among French property-owners.

The Republic without republicans

After the Commune a Catholic noble, Albert de Mun, who had
been taken prisoner by the Prussians at Metz and then released
to help with its suppression, observed that the Republic 'seemed
dishonoured for ever'. A great chance to restore the monarchy
presented itself. Many conservatives believed that only the
monarchy could guarantee religion, the family and private property. The National Assembly repealed the law of exile which
banned heads of the royal families; and the two pretenders – the
Comte de Chambord and the Comte de Paris, respectively grand-
sons of Charles X and Louis-Philippe, Legitimist and Orleanist
– returned to France (**11**).

However, things were not so simple. The reason given by many
historians for the failure of restoration at this point is that on 5 July
1871 the Comte de Chambord, who had spent most of his life in
exile in Austria, issued a manifesto saying that he would never give
up the white flag of Henri IV (which in any case had been
regularly used as the royal flag only since 1815) [**doc. 2a**]. But the
explanation cannot be reduced to the foibles of one man. Royalists
included politicians as well as pretenders. The problem was that
Chambord failed to consult with the grand old man of royalism
in France, the Comte de Falloux, who was obliged to deal in the
art of the possible. And in 1871 the plain fact was that only 80
deputies on the extreme Right of the National Assembly accepted
the manifesto (**12**); the so-called moderate Right and the centre
Right (or Orleanists) did not. Failure to consult was symptomatic
of something else: Chambord wanted the restoration of a 'real'
monarchy, which he variously called 'traditional', 'tutelary' or
'tempered'. It was not absolute monarchy, but it was not constitutional monarchy either. Unfortunately the vast majority of
royalist deputies wanted a constitutional, parliamentary monarchy
which left power in *their* hands. The lessons of 1830 and of the
authoritarian Empire had not been learned in vain [**doc. 2b**].

While the royalists argued amongst themselves, Gambetta was
stumping the country, delivering speeches and working to recreate
the image of the Republic. Above all it had to be dissociated from
that of the Commune. Gambetta claimed that the republicans were
the party of order; those who opposed the Republic presently
established were the sedition-mongers. Republicans did not
represent social revolution, he argued, because there was 'no social
question', no inevitable condition of class struggle. Society, for

Gambetta, was composed of 'individuals in a process of rising', climbing by means of education, thrift and sobriety towards the acquisition of property. Republicans were not the propertyless proletarians who had set Paris alight (indeed, Gambetta was careful to avoid the language of class) but rather the 'new social strata', the 'world of work', the tradesmen, small manufacturers and farmers who, he said, had been thrown up by the industrial revolution and universal suffrage (**13**).

The tide began to move in the direction of republicanism. Republicans did well in the by-elections of July 1871. Thiers, who was elected President of the Republic by the National Assembly, declared himself squarely in favour of the Republic at the beginning of the parliamentary session in November 1872. However, in order to retain a breadth of support on the Right, he declared, 'the Republic will be conservative, or it will not exist' [**doc. 3**]. His ideal was a presidential Republic, which vested most power in himself. Increasingly, the man who had negotiated peace and saved France from the Commune became suspect to the Right. They wanted not a presidential but a parliamentary constitution, under which ministers would be responsible to them. And they did not trust Thiers to be a strong enough bulwark against the rising tide of republicanism. The crunch came in April 1873, when in a by-election which polled the whole of Paris, Thiers's candidate, none other than his foreign minister, was defeated by the candidate of the radical Left, who had been approved by Gambetta. On 24 May 1873, Thiers was overturned by a majority composed of royalists and Bonapartists (**14**).

With Thiers gone there was again the possibility of a royalist restoration. The new president might have been the Orleanist Duc d'Aumale, but the (Legitimist) extreme Right objected, so the nomination went instead to a military man who had loyally served every regime since the Restoration, Marshal MacMahon. Nothing was settled yet. During the summer of 1873 royalist leaders were deep in conference. The Orleanist pretender, the Comte de Paris, agreed to defer to the claim of the Legitimist branch. The understanding was that he would succeed on the death of the Comte de Chambord, who was childless. But again Chambord slighted royalist notables by refusing to accept the tricolour, which was, after all, the flag not only of the Republic but of the constitutional monarchies of 1791 and 1830 and of the French army. Further, he refused to surrender his title in favour of the Orleanist branch, a gesture which would have saved his honour and France for the monarchy. In the absence of 'fusion', as the reconciliation of the claims of the rival branches was called, a consensus of conservatives was possible only *within* the Republic. On 20 November 1873 the royalist and Bonapartist majority in the National Assembly agreed to extend the presidential powers of MacMahon for seven years.

Chambord and the hard-line Legitimists were not the only obstacle to a royalist restoration. MacMahon took as his prime minister the Orleanist Duc de Broglie, and the Orleanists were anxious to establish a constitution as much like that of 1830 as possible. This would involve a Second Chamber that was largely appointed, and, in elections to the First Chamber, significant restrictions on universal suffrage. But democracy was too deeply entrenched and universal suffrage was untouchable in the eyes of both republicans and Bonapartists. De Broglie was toppled by an 'unholy' alliance of republicans, Bonapartists and Legitimists in May 1874. The Orleanists were now stranded. Moreover, they had reason to fear a revival of Bonapartism which, having been roundly beaten at the polls in 1871, won a series of by-elections in 1874. The Bonapartists argued that the Empire had been terminated by events; the people had not been consulted on the regime since 7.5 million had acclaimed the Liberal Empire in May 1870. They proposed the dissolution of the bickering National Assembly and a plebiscite which, they thought, would restore the Emperor's son, the Prince Imperial (**15**).

The Orleanists had no choice but to reach an understanding with moderate republicans on the establishment of a parliamentary republic which alone would keep Bonapartists, Legitimists and radicals out of power. It would be based on universal suffrage, but the Orleanists insisted on a Second Chamber as a condition of their support. This conjunction of centres was not extraordinary, but represented a natural coalition of talent, wealth and birth. Key negotiations took place between the Orleanist Duc d'Audiffret Pasquier and Auguste Casimir-Périer, a republican in the manner of Thiers, but the son of one of Louis-Philippe's prime ministers and Pasquier's brother-in-law and neighbour on the Champs Elysées. By February 1875 a constitution had been hammered out. There would be a Chamber of Deputies and a Senate, which together would elect a President of the Republic. The President had the right to dissolve the Chamber, but only with the approval of the Senate. The constitution of the Third Republic was unashamedly the fruit of compromise.

The Republic of the republicans

The constitution was firmly on paper; but it remained to be seen how it would operate in practice. In the first elections to the Chamber under the constitution, in February 1876, the republicans obtained a majority while the Orleanists, together with an alliance of Bonapartists and Legitimists, went down heavily. However, the Senate elected the previous month was in the hands of conservatives and conservative elements also dominated the magistracy, bureaucracy and army. This permitted MacMahon to appoint prime ministers not from the republican majority but from former ministers of Thiers, such as Jules Simon, who described himself as 'profoundly conservative and profoundly republican' (**16**). The principle of ministerial responsibility – that the composition of the ministry should reflect the parliamentary majority – was far from being established. This, however, was precisely what Gambetta and the republicans wished to establish. Gambetta indicted Simon's irresoluteness towards the pretensions of the Catholic Church – his famous cry was 'Clericalism, there is the enemy!' – in order to identify Simon with the Catholic Right and disqualify him as a republican. MacMahon, for his part, decided that Simon was not resolute enough against the pretensions of the republicans. On 16 May 1877 he dismissed Simon and replaced him with the Duc de Broglie, who formed a ministry of Orleanists and Bonapartists. The Chamber of Deputies was prorogued for a month and when it reconvened on 16 June it heard that the President had obtained the support of the Senate for the dissolution of the Chamber. This was within the letter of the constitution, but hardly in its spirit. The outraged republicans passed a vote of censure on the ministry by 363 votes to 158 [**doc. 4**].

Elections were held in October 1877. The government used all the means of pressure refined by the authoritarian Empire in order to break the republican majority. The republicans riposted by attacking the clericalism and Bonapartism of the government. The government failed. It took only 40 seats from the republicans who won an immense moral victory. MacMahon was obliged to admit one of the republican majority, Charles Freycinet, to the cabinet. The municipal elections of January 1878 were a 'town-hall revolution' with republicans sweeping to power in thousands of communes. Because senators were indirectly elected by colleges composed for the most part of mayors, the effect was felt when the Senate was renewed in January 1879. The republicans acquired a majority there as well. This was decisive. Marshal MacMahon resigned as President and the two chambers elected in his place a died-in-the-wool republican, the 71-year-old Jules Grévy.

The constitution of the Third Republic was established by compromise but compromise was no longer possible. The 16 May was regarded by the republicans as a *coup d'état* against the constitution, scarcely less evil than that of the 2 December 1851. Those who numbered among the 363 were immortalised as the preservers of republican legitimacy, crowned in glory. Those who had supported the coup were judged to have disqualified themselves for ever from office in the Republic. From now on, ministries were required to command not just a majority in the Chamber of Deputies but a majority of *republicans*. Politics in the Third Republic was henceforth to revolve around the strict principle of republican legitimacy: only legitimate republicans could claim to rule; the others were condemned to look on in impotence (**17**).

Part Two: Analysis

2 The Republic of the Notables

The President

The Third Republic was a parliamentary not a presidential Republic (**18**). The president was elected not directly by the people, as in 1848, but indirectly, by deputies and senators sitting together and assembled for that purpose at Versailles. This was clearly to prevent the emergence of another Bonaparte. (Direct presidential elections were not reintroduced until 1962.) By the same token the president was not responsible to the people, as Napoleon III had been – a position which conferred immense authority. Neither was he responsible to parliament, as Thiers had been in 1871. This was the position of ministers. It was impossible for parliament to force a president to resign; however a ministerial 'strike' or collective refusal to serve in a cabinet under him could achieve this by another route. The president had the right to dissolve the Chamber of Deputies, if he had the agreement of the Senate, but no president attempted this after 16 May 1877; the lesson had been learned. Even so, the powers of the president were not negligible. He had the direction of foreign policy: the Franco-Russian alliance was very much the personal triumph of Sadi Carnot. The president chose the president of the council of ministers (the technical name for the prime minister): Grévy was able to keep out an extremist like Gambetta and prefer a moderate like Freycinet until the shift to the left in the elections of 1881 forced his hand. Even then, Gambetta was allowed to do his worst and fell after two months. The president was also able to exert pressure to influence the composition of cabinets: Grévy insisted that ministries reflect not only the parliamentary majority but also the temper of the country as a whole (**19**).

Ministries

Parliament was the constitutional centre of gravity in the Third Republic. This was a deliberate rehabilitation following the Second Empire, when it had been firmly subordinated to the executive.

Deputies had the right to interpellate ministries – that is, to demand an account of men and measures – and to propose votes of no confidence. This tended to produce a rapid turnover of ministries: there were 108 between 1870 and 1940, averaging eight months each. Such statistics seem to support the thesis of ministerial instability in the Third Republic. But factors promoting stability must also be examined. The fall of a ministry did not entail a general election, only the formation of a new ministry. A 'new' ministry was often only a 'replastering' of the old one, with the introduction of some ministers to reflect the colour of the victorious majority, but the carrying-over of many old faces too. In the period of the so-called Opportunist Republic (1879–93), a pool of no more than six or seven ministers formed the basis of almost every ministry. Recognised *ministrables* – those clearly eligible for office – constantly shadowed those actually in office. And while ministries rose and fell, ministers often had very long careers. Thus Freycinet was continuously in office between 1888 and 1893, as was Delcassé between 1898 and 1905 (**20**).

Ministries were responsible to parliament, and had to command a majority there to survive. The invocation of the principle of republican legitimacy required more specifically that a majority of republican deputies support it. This ruled out the possibility of *alternance* between ministries of the Left and ministries of the Right. Even if there were a dominance of centrist feeling in the country at large, this could not be translated into a conjunction of centres in parliament. The consensus of 1875 had been destroyed by the crisis of 16 May 1877. Ministries which were seen to rely on the votes of the Right, such as that of Rouvier in 1887 or Méline in 1896, were fiercely challenged in the Chamber. The role of the Senate was less clear. After 16 May, when it had approved the presidential coup, it was confined to a subordinate position. Yet it was not a negligible factor. It managed to topple the radical ministry of Léon Bourgeois in 1896, even though Bourgeois had a majority in the Chamber.

The Senate

The Senate was a present given to the Orleanists in return for their acceptance of universal suffrage. A single chamber brought back memories of the Convention parliament of 1792, forum of the Jacobins and a prey to radical clubs and popular demonstrations, even though single chambers in 1849 and 1871 had been dominated by royalists. The Senate was to provide some insulation of the political system against overheating by universal suffrage. It was elected indirectly by colleges of mayors and councillors of departmental and *arrondissement* assemblies. The countryside and small towns were over-represented in the Senate, while large towns were under-represented, which gave rise to the epithet the 'Chamber of Agriculture'. Senators were elected for nine years (as against four years for deputies), the Senate being renewed by a third every three years, to ensure continuity. This meant that an outgoing senator might be thirteen or fifteen years on from a direct consultation of the people. The republicans refused to accept the Orleanists' desire for nominated senators, but one-quarter of the Senate were originally elected as life-senators. This system was terminated in 1884, though life-senators in post were allowed to continue for life.

Although it occupied second place to the Chamber, the Senate was not powerless. Its majority after 1879 was republican, but it was above all a centrist majority which disliked extremes. It stood out against anticlerical legislation, progressive income tax and parliamentary reform. Jules Ferry called it the 'fortress of the Republic', by which he meant that it offered stout resistance to the tyranny of popular opinion, and in particular to public opinion whipped up by demagogues like Boulanger. The Senate provided a secure and honourable retirement for politicians, but in its own right nurtured leaders of the nation. Between 1898 and 1914 it provided eight of the thirteen presidents of the council and three presidents of the Republic: Loubet, Fallières and Poincaré (**21**).

The Chamber of Deputies

The Chamber of Deputies was directly elected by universal manhood suffrage. In 1871 this operated under a system of departmental proportional representation, which obliged candidates to present themselves on a list (the so-called *scrutin de liste*). This gave way in 1875 to a system of single-member constituencies, of which there might be four, six or eight to a department. Such constituencies had a tendency to become 'fiefs' of sitting deputies, who were often local men who had come up through the regular channel of mayor and departmental councillor before their election to parliament (**22**). Two-thirds of all deputies between 1870 and 1940 held on to their seats for an average period of fourteen years (**23**). This system was detested by Gambetta and the radical republicans, who argued that only the restoration of the *scrutin de liste* would force deputies to bow to the discipline of an organised republican party. In 1885 the departmental lists were tried again, but this had the effect of increasing the representation of radicals and conservatives at the expense of moderate republicans, and then of allowing Boulangism to gain a hold. The single-member constituencies were restored in 1889.

Under the Second Empire (and in 1877) the Ministry of the Interior and the prefects – the government's agents in each department – tended to promote 'official candidates' who were well-disposed to the government and managed the elections for them. Under the Third Republic influence shifted towards the deputies (**24**). Ministries needed their support in votes of confidence, and had to deal with them individually, because there were no organised parties. Deputies were prepared to give that support in exchange for favours for their constituents, to help the process of re-election. Such favours included scholarships at the local *lycée*, exemption from compulsory military service, jobs ranging from a prefectship to running a tobacconist's shop (tobacco was a government monopoly), the suspension of judicial proceedings against cafés for infringing the licensing laws (cafés were often centres of political meeting and support), and contracts and concessions for railway companies and other businesses. The government was not wholly without influence. 'Ministerial' deputies obtained favours; those opposed to the ministry did not, and had to use other means to secure constituents' votes, such as the threat of eviction from farms or harnessing the support of the clergy. It was not unknown for the children of those who voted against the local landowner to be prohibited from taking their First Communion.

The republican notables of 1880 were most unlike the republican militants who were punished after Louis-Napoleon's *coup d'état* in 1851. In the southern department of the Gard the vast majority of the militants had been peasants, artisans and intellectuals, while 74 per cent of the notables were landowners, merchants, industrialists, professional men or civil servants. As the Republic became established, so republicanism became more bourgeois. The profile of deputies in 1877 and 1885 confirms this picture: 89 per cent came from the same landed, business, professional and official categories. Similar social backgrounds often meant that friendships were formed across political barriers. The Palais Bourbon was something of a club. As Robert de Jouvenel said in 1914, 'There is less difference between two deputies, one of whom is a revolutionary and the other not, than between two revolutionaries, one of whom is a deputy and the other not' (**24a**).

Despite the distinctly bourgeois nature of deputies, they were not in a very easy position financially. The salary was a meagre 9,000 francs after 1871 – less than they had been paid under the Second Empire and equivalent to the salary of a tax inspector, a colonel in the artillery or a headmaster of a Paris lycée (a senior prefect might earn 35,000 francs in 1880). Deputies' salaries rose to 15,000 francs only in 1907, when ministers were paid a handsome 60,000 francs. The other side of their independence from party discipline was the lack of expenses from any party to fight elections. And the cost of elections, of course, was very high. Control of a local newspaper to put across their views was essential for deputies. Most canvassing took place in cafés and the candidate was expected to be generous. At election time it helped to give charity to hospitals, compensate communes for flood-damage or buy new uniforms for the firemen. Here is the root of what has often been dismissed as the corruption and venality of Third Republic politicians (**25**) [**doc. 5**]. Given the huge bills they had to meet, it was attractive to them to be offered funds or directorships by financial, industrial or colonial enterprises which were themselves seeking contacts and concessions from the government. Business, the press and politics interlocked very closely under the Third Republic.

The commune

The 36,000 communes were the cells of French political life. Each commune had its mayor and municipal council, with the exception of Paris, which had a municipal council but no mayor. In the municipal elections of 1878 and 1881 the republicans came to power in thousands of communes. However, in spite of Gambetta's gestures towards the 'new social strata', little of a social revolution was entailed. At Mazières-en-Gâtine, a small commune in the west of France, for example, the royalist mayor, the Vicomte de Tusseau, heir of the pre-revolutionary seigneurs, was displaced in 1881 by a republican, M. Proust. But Proust, the son-in-law of a doctor and belonging to an established local family, was described as 'from a social point of view, resolutely conservative' (**26**). One system of patronage followed another, spoils went to new clients and the petty politics of village life continued.

The presence of clientelism is sometimes taken to exclude politics. It is often argued too that rural populations were ignorant of or indifferent to national issues. This was not the case. The burning question of the 1880s was whether religious congregations or lay teachers should teach in the schools maintained by communes, while that of the 1900s was whether the congregations, expelled from the communal schools, should be allowed to run their own private schools. These controversies linked every commune in France to political battles going on in parliament, and ensured that the axis of French politics, which divided anticlerical from clerical, republican from conservative, blue from white (to use the terms forged during the French Revolution), ran through every region of France, dividing commune from commune and sometimes, within the commune, family from family (**27**). The irony was that the school question, by polarising politics along religious lines, and clienteles respectively behind conservative and republican notables (thus hindering the emergence of social issues and the polarisation of politics along class lines), actually promoted stability in the Third Republic.

3 Left and Right

For the first thirty years of the Republic the question of the legitimacy of the Republic underscored the essential difference between Left and Right. The school question, dividing anticlerical from clerical, was really a battle for the survival of the Republic. The question of the working class was subordinated to this higher cause: their grievances could not be attended to so long as the existence of the regime was in doubt. Similarly, the nascent movement to claim equal rights of citizenship for women could find no space to express itself. Indeed, because women's organisations were persecuted alongside radical and socialist ones by the conservative governments of the mid-1870s, women's leaders tended of their own accord to put the defence of the anticlerical Republic first (**28**).

However neither Right nor Left was monolithic. On the republican side there were men of 1848 who had been persecuted after 1851, veterans of the Paris Commune (many in exile of a forced or voluntary nature before 1880), patriots of 1870, and those who had rallied late in the day from Bonapartism or Orleanism. In the 1880s they tended to fall into two main camps, the moderates or Opportunists, and the radicals. On many issues they divided, but in the last resort, when the republican principle itself was threatened, they pulled together under the slogan of 'republican concentration'. The Right was fragmented in its own way. One problem was dynastic, in that there were three rival monarchical claims: Legitimist, Orleanist and Bonapartist. More subtly, there were differences between those who were irreducibly opposed to the Republic as such, and those who were prepared to compromise with the regime, so long as they were given a chance to enter a governing majority, influence policy and one day themselves hold office. Unfortunately the principle of republican legitimacy ruled this out of order. The Right was condemned to exclusion on what seemed to be a permanent basis. The pattern of politics which now became a risk was the following: that the moderate republicans or Opportunists would find themselves isolated from the radicals, and though inclined for practical reasons to seek accommodation with the moderate Right be prohibited by their own principles from doing so. A corollary of this was that an alliance of some sort might be formed between radicals and the Right, for they had at least one thing in common: a desire to get the Opportunists out of power. This alliance in the late 1880s took the form of Boulangism.

The enemies of Opportunism

On the left wing of the republican movement were the radicals. They attacked the Opportunists who, anxious to distance themselves from any association with the Commune, refused to amnesty the Communards until 'the opportune time'. This turned out to be in June 1880, when the Opportunists thought that the country was ready, and that any controversy could be out of the way well before the elections of 1881 (**29**). The radicals were highly critical of the constitution of 1875 and determined to revise it. For them it was republican only in name, and in no sense gave power to the people. They wanted the abolition of the Senate, deputies to be bound by imperative mandates, and the executive to be a mere agent of parliament. Some concessions were tossed in their direction – the abolition of life-senators in 1884, the restoration of the *scrutin de liste* in 1885 – but not enough to satisfy them. Radicals were also strict anticlericals who demanded the exclusion of religious congregations from education and the Separation of Church and State (the Catholic Church, having been deprived of its property at the Revolution, was maintained by the state under the Concordat of 1801). Gambetta adopted the rhetoric of militant anticlericalism to please them, especially when he toured the Midi [**doc. 6a**]. But the man to do something as Minister of Education was Jules Ferry, and although Ferry was the architect of free, compulsory, lay public primary education in 1881–2, he believed in a working compromise with the Catholic Church, notably with regard to the Concordat and the education of girls [**doc. 6b**]. Moreover, while the catechism was no longer taught in state primary schools after 1882, it was replaced by a secular morality which offered just as many guarantees of social order.

Radicals differed from Opportunists also in the priority they gave to social reform. They pressed for the nationalisation of the railway companies, whereas the Opportunist government preferred to expand the railway network in conjunction with the 'big six' railway companies, funding them and guaranteeing the loans they

17

raised (**30**). The radicals wanted free trade, in order to provide cheap food for workers; the Opportunists agreed to 'Corn Laws' in 1885 for the benefit of landowners (**31**). Radicals demanded rights for trade unions, which were indeed conceded in 1884, but with the aim, in the government's eyes, of separating organised labour from socialist agitators. The last bone of contention was foreign policy. Establishing colonies in North Africa and Indo-China was the Opportunists' way of redeeming national honour without antagonising Bismarck. Radicals were unimpressed. They argued that colonies served the interests of banks, railway companies, the steel industry and arms manufacturers, while ordinary Frenchmen had to pay the taxes and fight the battles. More than that, they adopted a patriotic stance, pointing out that Germany was the real enemy, and must be faced in the Vosges, not in Vietnam (**32**). Outside parliament a *Ligue des Patriotes* was set up by Paul Déroulède in 1882 to mobilise veterans, educate youth in the patriotic spirit, press for *revanche* (revenge) against Germany and generally embarrass the Opportunist oligarchy (**33**). Inside parliament the radical leader, Georges Clemenceau, managed to bring down Opportunist ministries on three colonial entanglements, in Tunisia, Egypt and Indo-China (**34**).

The radicals did not have the numbers to do this on their own. But the Right also disliked colonial policies which were costly and could lead to war, and were prepared to vote with radicals in order to topple Opportunist ministries. Conservatives and Opportunists were at daggers drawn in other ways. As grain prices fell in the 1880s, bringing down rents and land values as well, so the agricultural interest lobbied for protection. This became a powerful force behind the recovery of the Right, and the Opportunists were wise to concede a protective agricultural tariff in May 1885, just before the elections (**35**). Equally capable of mobilising votes was resistance to the anticlerical policies of Jules Ferry. Conservatives linked the defence of Catholic schools to the defence of religion and social order in general, and through the school question assured themselves of the support of the clergy as electoral agents, especially in regions of high religious practice. The constitutional issue had been a liability for the Right, but now things were changing. In 1878 Albert de Mun had dared to salute an 'imminent counter-revolution'. He was firmly slapped down by the royalist leader, the Comte de Falloux (**36**). Softly, softly was the order of the day. The death of the Comte de Chambord in 1883 made possible a Union of the Right headed by a former Bonapartist, the Baron de Mackau. This Union was still against the Republic, but the term 'conservative' was now used in preference to 'royalist', to maintain the option of accommodation with the regime.

The Bonapartists could not yet be discounted but were rather confused about strategy. They divided between those who ran with the royalists, to defend Catholic and conservative interests, and those who accepted that, by elections if not by plebiscite, the people had been consulted, and had declared themselves in favour of the Republic. For the latter, the option was to join with radicals who were dissatisfied with the Opportunist Republic, and to seek revision of the constitution. This wing rallied round Prince Jérôme Napoleon (nicknamed Plon-Plon), cousin of the late Emperor, who became the Bonapartist claimant after the death of the Prince Imperial in 1879, killed while fighting in South Africa. The conservative wing detested Prince Napoleon as a maverick radical, and after 1883 tried to hijack his son, Prince Victor, just out of military college, for their cause. They were much less happy with the Republic and had links with royalists.

Opportunism between Left and Right

The elections of October 1885 threw the political system into disarray. The rule was a two-ballot system: if a candidate or (in 1885–9) a list failed to obtain an overall majority at the first ballot, a run-off would be held. Some candidates would see fit to withdraw and instruct their supporters to vote for a political ally. This made for all sorts of negotiations and coalitions between the ballots. The first ballot in 1885 was a free-for-all. Radicals as well as conservatives ran against the Opportunists. The result was extremely worrying: republicans won 129 seats by absolute majority, but conservatives won 176. Radicals and Opportunists faced the possibility of a return to the non-republican majority of 1871–6, with dire consequences. They had to sink their differences in the second ballot and subscribe to 'republican concentration'. As a result republicans won 254 seats at the second ballot and conservatives only 25.

The republicans retained their majority, but for the Opportunists the situation was not happy. They numbered 201 in the new Chamber against 180 radicals and far Left and 203 conservatives (including about 100 royalists and 50 Bonapartists). They had survived only by courtesy of the radicals and for the first time had to concede ministerial posts to them. President Grévy refused to take the radical Floquet as prime minister, but took Freycinet along with prominent radicals, such as René Goblet as Education Minister and General Georges Boulanger, a protégé of Clemenceau, as Minister of War. The radicals forced through their own policies. Religious congregations were expelled from state primary schools. After the marriage of the daughter of the Comte de Paris to the Crown Prince of Portugal in Paris in May 1886, which looked like a gathering of the Orleanist court, a law was passed exiling the heads and heirs of previous reigning families. Boulanger started to republicanise the army, where the officer corps was still very royalist and imperialist. Four Orleanist princes were relieved of their commands, royalist garrisons were shifted into republican towns, and a new military law (eventually passed in 1889) imposed three years' service on all young men, ending exemption for seminarists and the wealthy.

Boulanger's special turn was to threaten *revanche* against Germany, to the delight of his revolutionary-patriotic supporters. However, Bismarck took his threats seriously, called up the reserve and (after new elections) had the Reichstag agree to enlarge the German army. This frightened the Opportunists, and to avert the danger of war they allied with the Right to overthrow the radical-infested ministry and Boulanger with it. Already the rules of republican legitimacy were being bent. Would it go any further? There were moderates on the Right who wanted nothing better than to form a ruling alliance with moderate republicans against the radicals. One of them, the Bonapartist deputy Edgar Raoul-Duval, had launched a paper in November 1886 (shortly after the Whigs had defected to the Tories in Great Britain in opposition to Irish Home Rule) in which he asked, 'Why can't we have *our* Whigs and Tories?' (**37**). In the crisis following the fall of Boulanger, Grévy consulted with the leader of the Union of the Right, Baron de Mackau, who said that the Right would support any moderate cabinet in which Boulanger did not figure. A ministry was formed by the banker, Maurice Rouvier, which claimed to be based on a republican majority. But as far as the radicals were concerned, it was a 'German' ministry, arranged to please Bismarck, which held on to power only with the support of the Right. The radicals decided to detach the Right from both Rouvier and Grévy, in whom they had lost confidence. A scandal was exposed. Grévy's son-in-law, Daniel Wilson, was accused of managing an agency in the Elysée Palace which sold recommendations for honours, and was arrested. Since the President was not formally responsible, the radicals secured the help of the Right to topple Rouvier (November 1887) and then organised a boycott of ministers. Freycinet, Goblet and Clemenceau (even he was asked) declined to form a cabinet. Grévy was obliged to resign (**38**).

The task in December 1887 was to find a new president. The front-runner was Jules Ferry, but because he was the Opportunist Republic incarnate, he aroused intense hostility. The radicals disliked his devotion to the Senate and knew that he regretted the effective loss of the president's power of dissolution, by using which the impossible Chamber of 1885 would have gone long ago. The conservatives hated his anticlerical legislation. Both sides opposed his colonial policies. Radicals and conservatives had to agree on a candidate to keep out Ferry. Floquet was not acceptable to the conservatives; Freycinet was not acceptable to the radicals. They settled for an outsider, Sadi Carnot, who belonged to a dynasty of republican technicians, grandson of the 'organiser of victory' in the French revolutionary wars.

Revenge of the disinherited: Boulangism

The exclusion of Ferry did not satisfy radicals or conservatives for long. They wanted to have done with the Opportunist Republic. After the Wilson scandal and the fall of Grévy it seemed vulnerable; and in Boulanger they had a stick to beat it with. Boulanger was adopted as a champion by the disinherited on both Right and Left, although for some time the left hand did not know what the right was doing (**39**).

An early interest in Boulanger was shown by Bonapartists who had dropped the hereditary principle (not least because it was discredited by the row between Prince Napoleon and Prince Victor) and accepted the Republic as a form of government, but wanted to revise the constitution. In particular, they wanted to establish the direct election of the president of the Republic; after all, that was how Louis-Napoleon had started in 1848. In January 1888 a Bonapartist journalist, Georges Thiébaud, introduced Boulanger to Prince Napoleon in Switzerland. Each denied that he was personally interested in running for the presidency, although the prince later admitted that Boulanger was 'a nail to hang your coat on'. Meanwhile a Bonapartist cable-magnate, Count Dillon, realised that they would have to look to the royalist camp for funds. For his part the Comte de Paris concluded that after a string of electoral defeats a plebiscite in the Bonapartist manner offered the best chance of success, appealing to the people over the heads of parties and politicians. Royalist leaders such as Mackau and Albert de Mun were ready to try Boulanger. The Duchesse d'Uzès, whom Boulanger as War Minister had once called on in order to apologise for a subordinate's refusal to allow her to hunt in the forest of Rambouillet, was happy to provide funds. As a later exposure of the affair had it, 'for the royalists the general is a card; for the general, royalism is a bank' (**40**).

All these negotiations went on in the deepest secrecy. Publicly, Boulanger was seen to be a man of the Left. He was promoted by radicals and members of the extreme Left like the former Communard, Henri Rochefort. Déroulède's *Ligue des Patriotes* acted as an extra-parliamentary organisation for Boulangism. In parliament, one of the radical Boulangists, Laguerre, demanded the revision of the constitution on 30 March. He provoked the fall of the ministry and its replacement by one under Floquet, who was known to favour revision. Boulanger was sent on a campaign of by-elections quite shamelessly as a media attraction. Under the list system a whole department had to be polled when one seat fell vacant. Boulanger presented his candidature, fought the election, resigned, and moved on to the next contest. He both seduced and repelled the Left. It was impossible to be sure what he stood for. He divided radicals, socialists and Blanquists down the middle: some issued grave warnings, others jumped on to the bandwagon. What was incontestable was his massive popular appeal. The socialist militants of Bordeaux, sensing the mood of the unemployed dock workers, threw in their lot with Boulanger. The support he received in the mining communities of the Nord department where he stood in April 1888 has been described as 'an explosion of working-class discontent' (**41**).

Gradually, rumours about the General's links with the Right leaked out. More and more activists on the Left worried that Boulanger would not make the Republic more responsive to the people but turn out to be a new Bonaparte. In May 1888 a Society of the Rights of Man was set up by a group of radicals, socialists and Opportunists to fight him. In July, Boulanger decided to take up a seat in the Chamber and called for its dissolution. Floquet, the prime minister, attacked him for having 'passed from sacristies to the antechambers of princes'. Boulanger's republicanism was openly impugned. He challenged Floquet to a duel, but it was the white-haired premier who wounded the General in the throat.

These revelations made the conservatives happier with Boulanger, and they increased their support for him in a number of by-elections held in August. Republicans drew further back and attacked him as a reactionary and a Bonapartist. Boulanger replied to his accusers in a speech on the anniversary of Louis-Napoleon's *coup*, 2 December 1888. He was not a Bonapartist, he insisted, for Louis-Napoleon had restricted liberty and restored monarchical power. On the other hand, he favoured not an intransigent, closed Republic but 'a new, national Republic, open to all decent men' [**doc. 7**]. This, in fact, was exactly what republicans feared: a hole punched in the principle of legitimacy which would end their monopoly of power and make way for a ruling majority in which the Right could participate.

Boulanger had one more chance. Floquet challenged him to fight a by-election in Paris in January 1889. Unfortunately, it was impossible to construct a complete republican alliance against Boulanger. The republican candidate represented the radicals and Opportunists but the socialists ran their own man and one wing of the Blanquists continued to support Boulanger in harness with the conservatives. Boulanger was thus able to draw support from the working-class suburbs of Paris as well as from the wealthy western districts, and he won the election.

The tolerance of the Third Republic could not be tried too far. Machinery was smartly activated to deal with the problem. The *Ligue des Patriotes*, which had organised the rank-and-file of Boulangism, was dissolved. Déroulède and Laguerre were prosecuted. Boulanger, Rochefort and Dillon, all of whom fled, were condemned *in absentia* by the Senate sitting as a High Court. The electoral system which had allowed Boulangism to flourish was altered: single-member constituencies were brought back in February 1889 and the right to stand in several constituencies at once was ended that August. In the elections of October 1889 monarchists, Bonapartists and Boulangists were all put in their place, with 210 seats to the republicans' 366. The Republic was secure for the moment, but a new force was emerging to cause concern: socialism.

4 Social Structure

The political system of the Third Republic cannot be studied in isolation from its social structure. Social strains or conflicts have immediate political repercussions. Land hunger in Russia, the declining petty bourgeoisie in Germany, and the toughness of the oligarchy in Spain were structural factors which in part explain the Revolution of 1917, the National Socialist seizure of power in 1933, and the Spanish Civil War. French society, partly because of the achievements of the Revolution of 1789, partly because of the slow, steady nature of its economic growth, was comparatively harmonious. It may be, to reverse the argument, that the very stability of French society permitted the luxury of sharp political divisions.

The peasantry

The countryside weighed heavily in French life. The total population in 1901 was 39 millions, of whom 23 millions lived in rural areas (defined as communes with an agglomerated population of under 2,000) and 16 millions worked in agriculture. The pace of change was slow: in 1846 the rural population had been 27 millions and the agricultural population 20 millions, while as late as 1931 the rural population was 20 millions and the agricultural population 11 millions. Fears were expressed at the turn of the century about rural depopulation. In fact the countryside remained healthily populated; far more significant was the shift away from agricultural activity (**42**).

Social stratification in the countryside was far less sharp than in the countries of southern and eastern Europe. France was a country of small farms rather than of large estates and an agricultural proletariat. Properties under 5 hectares accounted for 71 per cent of properties and 14 per cent of the land surface in France in 1892, which may be compared to 54 per cent of properties and 6 per cent of the land surface in Hungary in 1895. Peasants were considerable landholders in their own right: 45 per cent of properties were owner-occupied in 1892, and peasant-proprietors rented out additional land from landowners to work themselves (**43**). There were middlemen who made conditions worse for peasants in a few cases. In the Allier department farmers-general leased land and sublet it to *métayers* (share-croppers) along with seed, live-stock and tools, for which they exacted half the crop, various dues and cartage duties. And in the centre of France (Nièvre, Cher, Yonne) timber-merchants leased forest land and hired bands of woodcutters, both permanent and seasonal, at very low rates to clear it. However, these forms of exploitation were confined to specific areas of France.

The opening up of agricultural land in Russia and the United States and the improvement of transport by steamship and railway drove down farm prices between 1875 and 1900 in France by 27 per cent for cereals and 19 per cent for meat. This reduced the capital value of land by (on average) a third between 1879 and 1912. But the pressure was taken off tenant-farmers, who obtained lower rents and longer tenures (even if they were not indemnified for improvements made to the farm when they left or were evicted), and also off agricultural labourers and farm-hands, whose wages rose significantly at the end of the century. The agricultural interest secured protection against cheap imports of cereals, meat and wine under tariffs of 1885 and 1892. This spared them the need to modernise agriculture radically. On the other hand there was an increase in agricultural productivity as a result of mechan-isation to save on expensive labour (threshing machines, horse-drawn reapers and, on the eve of the war, the first reaper-binders) and the use of chemical fertilisers to improve yields. The decline of grain and meat prices and the growth of urban markets supplied by railway encouraged different forms of specialisation. These included dairy farming (for milk, butter and cheese) in Normandy, Brittany, the Centre and Poitou-Charentes, sugar-beet in the North-East and wine along the Mediterranean coast (**44**). The phylloxera epidemic of the early 1880s destroyed most of the vines, but production recovered so rapidly after replanting that wine prices fell by 50 per cent between the 1880s and 1900–7 (**45**).

One historian of this subject has called his book 'The Class Struggle in the Countryside' (**46**). Certainly there were cases of rural strikes and unionisation, notably of the woodcutters of the Centre in 1891–2, the winegrowing proletariat of the south in 1904 and 1907 and the *métayers* of the Allier (almost) in 1909. But several qualifications must be made. First, peasants as tenants and owners were far more concerned by prices and rents than by wages. The

25

leaders of the Federation of Land Workers in the Allier thus guided the *métayers* away from strike action towards the acquisition of a 'charter' or model lease for share-croppers; towards co-operatives to buy seeds and fertilisers, to provide credit and insurance and to market their goods; and towards professional and general education (**47**). Second, rural hierarchies persisted, not least because co-operatives were often funded and taken over by landowners, who insisted that they were the instruments of 'social peace' in the 'agricultural class' as a whole, as opposed to the class organisations of the towns. Lastly, as we have seen, the triumph of the republicans in the countryside served only to replace one set of rural notables by another. Peasants made up two-thirds of the electorate but the main political battle was between anticlericalism and clericalism, which obliged the rural populations to line up behind republican or Catholic-conservative notables, with little chance to air their own grievances (**48**).

Workers

The size of France's proletariat must be put in perspective (**49**). The number of industrial workers increased between 1886 and 1911 from 3 millions to 4.75 millions, but in 1911 the active industrial population was only 33 per cent of the total active population as against 41 per cent in agriculture. It was far from being urban in any hardened sense. Industrial workers were recruited from the countryside, although many rural migrants went to the large towns but not into industry. Often they came from declining rural industries such as handloom weaving or charcoal-fired metallurgy. It should not be forgotten that women made up 30 per cent of the industrial workforce in 1866, rising to 38 per cent in 1911. This is not surprising, because on average they were paid less than half the male wage (**50**). Statistics for 1906 show that they were concentrated in the clothing industry (1.4 million women, 89 per cent of the workforce) and textiles (0.5 million, 56 per cent). This may be compared to domestic service (0.75 million, 77 per cent) and agriculture (3.3 millions, 38 per cent of the workforce) (**51**). The number of foreign immigrants – Belgians, joined towards the end of the century by Italians and Spaniards – reached one million (2.8 per cent of the population) in 1911. Since the immigrants were ready to take low-paid jobs, they were often seen as a threat to the native workforce: a dozen Italians were killed at Aigues-Mortes on the Mediterranean coast in 1893. Although a growing number of workers were born and brought up in large towns, many could be described as semi-rural. They returned to the land for the harvest, as the silk-workers of Lyon did to pick grapes in the Beaujolais, or, like two-thirds of the miners of Carmaux in the South-West in 1856–1913, they owned small properties which they still worked (**52**). For these workers, industrial work was often seen as a stage to increase their earnings before they returned to cultivate the land.

The industrial system in France was very unlike the Russian model of large factories and a concentrated proletariat. Of course there were large textile mills, coal mines and metallurgical plants but the average size of a firm was small: 2.6 workers in 1866, 3.2 workers in 1896, falling again to 2.7 workers in 1906. Despite the abolition of the guilds at the Revolution the tradition of the artisan lived on, helped by French excellence in luxury industries, by long apprenticeships which still existed in trades such as printing, engraving, jewellery and cabinet-making, and by what Jules Ferry called in 1881 'the magnificent union of craft and art' (**27**, p. 340).

The demand for cheap, mass-produced goods was nevertheless undermining this seemingly idyllic world. Protection was less effective for industry than for agriculture and productivity therefore became the key to survival. The working day was long, and a law of 1892 which established an 11-hour maximum for women over 18 was widely ignored. Where it was not, as in the textile mills, female workers suffered wage-cuts, although they often went on strike in protest. The mechanisation of processes from silk-weaving and watch-making to the manufacture of boots and shoes took place later in France than in Great Britain, and with painful results. It made craft-skills dispensable, eroded the long years of apprenticeship which (in the absence of guilds) served to maintain the exclusiveness of trades, and made it possible to displace highly-paid skilled workers with lower-paid semi-skilled workers (**53**). On the other hand the development of new industries such as the machine-tool industry created an alternative demand for skilled workers to build and maintain the machines which were manned by less skilled operatives (**54**).

New kinds of labour organisation had to be developed in order to defend workers' interests. Trade unions, which were properly authorised in 1884 (in the minds of the legislators to detach workers from militant agitators), were able to put up a united front to employers in order to improve or defend wages and conditions, using the threat of strike action. The strike tended to be used offensively, to improve wages, in boom periods, by (skilled) printers, metal-workers and building workers; and defensively, to defend wages, in times of depression, by the 'big battalions' of weavers and miners (**55**). Unionisation rather lagged behind strike activity. The proportions of workers in various industries unionised by 1912 were 32 per cent in mining, 30 per cent in building, 27 per cent in transport and only 13 per cent in textiles (**56**). The total number in unions in 1913 was 1,027,000, which amounted to about 10 per cent of wage-earners, much less than the 26 per cent unionised at that time in Great Britain. There were only 89,300 women in trade unions at that time, not least because men often organised to enforce a closed shop against unskilled labour and female labour, which were seen as a threat to the wages and jobs of skilled male workers (**57**).

A union set up by a particular trade in one town was liable to be extremely vulnerable. Regional and then national federations of category unions were therefore organised. A national federation was achieved by the printers in 1881, the builders in 1882, the railway workers in 1890, the miners (after one attempt in 1883) in 1890 and the textile workers in 1891. But France was a large country and industrial conditions varied a great deal from one end to the other. The moderate, well-organised miners of the Nord and Pas-de-Calais, for example, refused to go along with the militant miners of the Centre and Midi when the latter called a strike in 1902, and they made a separate peace with the authorities (**58**). In general, unions federated into one body in a single town were far more effective than they were as members of category federations. This was the significance of the *Bourses du Travail*. These were labour exchanges, in which all local unions were represented, set up under the 1884 law to fight unemployment. They were subsidised by the municipality and could therefore afford to have one or two paid officials. In practice they were admirable unions of unions which founded new unions, increased the membership of old ones, amalgamated small craft-unions into larger industry-based ones, provided libraries for the self-education of the workforce and (not least) organised support among all unions for local strikes (**59**). In 1892 ten *Bourses du Travail* formed a national federation, which rivalled the national federation of category unions – the *Confédération Générale de Travail*, or CGT, which was set up in 1895.

The *petite bourgeoisie*

The *petite bourgeoisie*, known also as the '*classes moyennes*' and the 'new social strata' acclaimed by Gambetta, formed a thick wedge in French society between the masses and the elite (**60**). One gauge of its size was the 23 per cent of the active population engaged in commerce, banking, transport and services in 1911 (the proportion in Italy at the same time was only 16 per cent). Broadly speaking, the *petite bourgeoisie* could be divided into two sorts: '*la boutique*', or the small employers in commerce and industry, who had some capital but little education, and the white-collar workers (clerks or lower civil servants), who had some education but little or no capital.

The small employers were often themselves of popular origin. Miners dismissed for radical activities regularly became bar-owners. Peasants from the Auvergne formed a colony of 75,000 in Paris in the 1890s, making a living as rag-and-bone men or wine- and coal-merchants. In 1911, two in five Auvergnats in Paris were tradesmen, and every tenth tradesman and fifth café or hotel owner was an Auvergnat (or Auvergnate) (**61**). After 1880 the competition from large firms and department stores made life difficult for small tradesmen, and the Bretons who migrated to Paris at the end of the century were forced to find work as domestic servants or as labourers in railway yards, gasworks or tanning factories. On the other hand urbanisation created new clienteles. While the number of grocers in the smart 1st *arrondissement* of Paris fell from 131 to 60 between 1860 and 1914, squeezed out by the department stores, they rose from 196 to 456 in the working-class 20th *arrondissement* (**62**).

Shopkeeping was an unstable occupation but it was a good starting-point for employment in the more stable white-collar world. Social mobility was promoted by a number of factors. As children became less of an asset (as cheap labour) and more of a liability, so stricter birth-control was practised, pressing down the birth rate at the end of the century. This took place in the town before the country, and among the petty bourgeoisie before the working class. In the absence of National Insurance and a Welfare State the saving classes were sharply divided from the spending classes. The petty bourgeoisie were notoriously provident, putting their money into voluntary schemes to insure against sickness and old-age and to pay for a decent funeral. Above all there was the channel of education. After 1881 both elementary and higher primary education were free, but the desire to send children out to work early had to be balanced against the multiplication of jobs available to girls as well as boys who had some educational attainment. Between 1871 and 1912, for example, the number of posts in banking, shipping and insurance and on the railways increased from 71,000 to 310,000, those in the post office from 34,000 to 120,000, and those in public education from 110,000 to 180,000. The proportion of women in banking and commerce rose from 26 per cent in 1866 to 41 per cent in 1911. There were 13,000 female clerks, stenographers, typists and telephonists in the post office in 1913. Laicisation created posts in teaching and nursing which had previously been occupied by nuns. However, women accounted for only 8 per cent of pharmacists, 3 per cent of doctors and 0.3 per cent of lawyers in 1906.

The wages of clerks and minor civil servants lagged a long way behind their status, and while the professional organisation of white-collar workers in the private sector was fairly strong, in the public sector it was contested by the authorities. This was especially the case when civil service unions sought affiliation to the *Bourses du Travail* or CGT, which were considered to be revolutionary, or went on strike. When post office workers went on strike in 1906, for example, 500 of them were sacked.

The elite

The social elite in France included components of birth, wealth and education. The promotional power of education was a seductive myth, and was given practical reinforcement by the military service law of 1889, which exempted from two of the three years' service anyone with a degree from a faculty or diploma from a *grande école*. As a result the university population leaped from 17,000 in 1888 to 27,000 in 1896. However careers were far from automatically open to talent. The *baccalauréat* or secondary school leaving certificate was required to enter a faculty (and hence the professions), but secondary education, even in the state sector, was fee-paying. There were very few scholarships, and these usually went to the sons of civil servants. An education in Greek and Latin (not the newer, modern education) was needed to get into a law or medical faculty until 1902, and the general cultural skills required tended to penalise pupils from working-class backgrounds and women, at least until 1902, when the non-classical *baccalauréat* became an option (**63**). Regional universities were founded after 1893 but Paris was still the place to go to (in 1914 52 per cent of French medical students and 46 per cent of law and arts students were at Paris University), and this pushed up the cost of education still further (**64**).

Money still counted for a great deal in the determination of careers. Those from landed, financial and legal-bureaucratic back-grounds – the rich 'heirs' – attended the law faculties and mon-opolised the elite posts in the administration, magistracy and diplomatic corps (**65**). A meritocracy of those slightly less well-heeled but excelling in mathematics was recruited by competitive examination into the *grandes écoles* such as the Ecole Polytechnique. This was the gateway to top posts in the army, civil service and nationalised industries like the mines (graduates of the Ecole Polytechnique rarely patronised private industry before 1890). Young men of modest families who obtained scholarships at the *lycées* of the provinces and then went to arts faculties or to the Ecole Normale of Paris tended to become teachers in state secondary schools and higher education, where they had the status and salary of civil servants. Unfortunately there was also an 'intellectual proletariat', penniless, unable to finish their studies or, if they did, unable to find a job because of the 'overcrowding of the professions' regretted by contemporaries at the turn of the century. They had little choice but to make do as private tutors, school supervisors, copyists, translators or hack journalists, if they did not take to a life of crime or revolution (**66**).

One way of checking the overcrowding of professions and the passion for bureaucratic jobs (known as *fonctionnarisme*) was to develop the entrepreneurial spirit in the middle class. An additional incentive was the demand for managers and technicians set up by the expanding metallurgical, engineering and electrical industries. As capital needs increased and capital was raised through joint-stock companies and the stock market, so those who owned industry and those who managed it drifted apart and a good technical education became the main qualification for managers. To produce these managers, new schools of applied sciences and courses at provincial universities linked to local industries sprang up. However, the achievement of this professional education should not be exaggerated. Much of French industry, like textiles, was still based on the family firm, in which the entrepreneur's family provided both ownership and management (**67**, **68**). Commercial schools, which were supposed to train the next generation of importers and exporters, found that they could not place their graduates: most families engaged in foreign trade sent their sons abroad to gain experience.

Despite the passing of the nobility as a privileged status group the dominance of aristocratic values had not disappeared from French society. Many entrepreneurs still regarded business as a means to raise capital quickly prior to living off its revenue as a rentier. The bourgeoisie continued to invest in land and when they bought stocks and shares, chose those of a safe rather than speculative kind. France's aristocracy was not rigid and impenetrable like the Junkers of Prussia. Indeed its penury was forcing it to marry into great wealth. The industrialist Eugène Schneider married his four daughters into the nobility. Winaretta Singer, whose American father made a fortune from the invention of the sewing machine, married Prince Edmond de Polignac and became a leading society hostess. The monied bourgeoisie and the landed aristocracy amalgamated very much as a single plutocracy. This did not mean that there were no tensions in the upper echelons of society between parvenus and established nobles, provincial and Parisian nobles and pre-Revolution and imperial nobles. But the issue was one of snobbery rather than of substance. French nobles had no special claim to office or favour, like Prussian or Austrian nobles. France was a Republic, with no court other than the salons of the Faubourg Saint-Germain. The nobility were a social force, but of no consequence politically.

5 Socialism

French socialism had three main characteristics in this period. First, the labour movement did not gravitate spontaneously towards political action, that is, the acquisition of political power in order to reduce or abolish economic exploitation. It tended to distrust state power, and the politicians and parties who wielded it, and preferred to use a weapon over which it had direct control, the strike. Moreover, there was no single political party to which the movement could turn to further its aims. Socialist parties had a habit of quarrelling and fragmenting. In this sense the labour experience in France was rather different from that in Germany, where a single socialist party exercised hegemony over the trade union movement and steered it towards political action. Second, there was a tension in the French political tradition between revolution, which answered reactionary measures by barricades thrown together from paving stones in 1814, 1830, 1848 and 1871, and democracy, which invited socialist leaders to secure what they could by an appeal to universal suffrage. Third, it was possible for the socialist leaders to find political support outside the socialist movement proper, in the ranks of the democratic middle class. Both had a stake in defending the Republic and keeping it out of the hands of Catholics and conservatives. Jacobin rhetoric and practice bound them together. However, while there was no dissent on republican and anticlerical issues, as soon as issues of private property were raised the danger was that bourgeois and working-class elements would part company. Class conflict was more muted and diffuse in France than, say, in Spain, Germany or Russia, but it could never be ignored (**69**).

Party and class: political action and direct action

It must not be forgotten that the scars left by the Paris Commune took a long time to heal. More than that, the events of the Commune were preserved by the French working class as a myth, in order to define their identity as a pariah class, baptised by revolution and oppressed by the state. The execution and deportation of militants during and after the *Semaine Sanglante* separated the mass of Parisian workers from their leaders until the amnesty of 1880, and seemed to teach that it was better for them to keep their heads down, out of politics. Politics appeared to be dangerous; they also appeared to be corrupt and divisive. The socialist leader Jules Guesde set about founding a socialist party, although he said that 'against the political parties it is necessary, indispensable, to create a workers' party that is not political but socialist' (**69a**). By this he meant that the party should serve the interests of the workers themselves, not the ambitions of the party leaders. Guesde wanted to organise a party which would unite the working class, regardless of the political affiliations of individual workers. This he attempted at the third workers' congress, held at Marseille in October 1879 (**70**). A workers' party was set up, but only a fraction of the working class was represented – hatters and shoemakers, but not weavers, miners or foundry workers. Moreover the very different opinions within this artisan elite could not be reconciled. In particular anarchist sentiments were very strong among artisans and had been since the 1860s. They feared that Guesde's plans for the nationalisation of industry would result in the reinforcement of the authoritarian state, whereas they wanted workers themselves to take control of individual workshops and France to be a federation of autonomous communes. Disagreement led to the breakaway from Guesde's party first of the anarchists (in May 1881), then (in September 1882) of the followers of Paul Brousse, a former anarchist who wanted to free communes from the tutelage of the administration and enable communes conquered by socialists to take over local services such as gas and water. Brousse has often been referred to as a Possibilist, ready to settle for piecemeal, practical reforms, but the anarchist origins of his municipal socialism are quite clear (**71**).

In the early 1880s France was hit by depression and unemployment and working-class discontent increased. A large demonstration of the unemployed took place in Paris in March 1883 and a long strike, studied by Emile Zola for his novel *Germinal*, broke out in the mines of Anzin in February 1884. A mass base for socialism was taking shape. To prevent this, the Opportunist oligarchy decided in March 1884 to authorise trade unions fully (**72**). If unions were legal, it was argued, moderate workers would join them and they would no longer be the vehicle of extremists. Moreover, if the working class was able to improve its wages and conditions by bargaining, it would be less vulnerable to the blandishments of 'outside' socialist agitators. The government made sure of this by requiring unions to submit their statutes and the names of their officers to the authorities and by confining them to the pursuit of economic interests. The line between economic and political action was in fact difficult to draw (**59**). For example, republican municipalities often conceded *Bourses du Travail* to unions as a reward for their support in elections. This was said to be for purely 'economic' activity. But far from being simply a present to the workers, the *Bourses* were often wrested by the workers from their republican allies and were then used to strengthen their industrial muscle. The deviation of intentions soon became clear. When the *Bourse du Travail* of St Etienne backed the miners' strike in the Loire department in 1888, the radical mayor and council, which had funded it, decided that this action was political (that is, not to their taste), and dissolved the *Bourse*. Further, although the government had authorised trade unions, this did not prevent employers from refusing to negotiate with them or from sacking workers because they belonged to them. This often forced unions to resort to political action. The miners and glass-workers of Carmaux won the municipality from the conservatives, who represented the mine-owners, in May 1892. The authorities then dismissed the socialist mayor, and the miners responded by launching a strike which lasted from August to November 1892. The strike forced the resignation of the conservative deputy, an aristocratic mine-owner, and in the by-election of January 1893, Jean Jaurès, professor at Toulouse University, then a radical, was sent by the miners to parliament. Now the miners had a tribune to represent them (**52**). Politics had come to their rescue.

The distinction between political and economic (or direct) action was eroded by some socialists and maintained by others for reasons of political advantage. Guesde's Workers' Party set up a National Federation of Trade Unions in 1886, gathering as many unions as possible, to transmit its ideology and to gear them to political activity – the conquest of political power by the Workers' Party. The Possibilists, known formally as the Federation of Socialist Workers of France, began to look more and more like a conventional political party. They won nine seats on the Paris municipal council in 1887, entered alliances with the ruling radicals, and opposed the navvies' strike of 1888. This disgusted Jean Allemane, who was an associate of Brousse, but had been deported for his activities during the Commune and had retained the intransigence of the Communards. His support lay among unskilled rather than skilled workers, who followed Brousse. From the premiss that 'the emancipation of the working class *can only* be by the workers themselves' (**72a**), he argued that their weapon must be the general strike, which would result in the transfer of workshops and worksites to workers' associations. His supporters broke with the Possibilists in 1890 and set up the Revolutionary Socialist Workers' Party. This captured the Paris *Bourse du Travail* from the Possibilists in 1891 and the following year organised a National Federation of *Bourses* (**73**). A bid was then made to break the hold of the Guesdists on the trade unions. In this the Allemanists were joined by the founders of the *Bourse* of St Nazaire, a young lawyer, Aristide Briand, and a journalist, Fernand Pelloutier, who also favoured the general strike (**74**). The Guesdists were opposed to the general strike because it erupted beyond their control and did not help the party to achieve political power. But Briand was able to obtain the support of the majority of delegates at the congress of the National Federation of Trade Unions at the end of 1892 for the general strike. The way was now open for the formation of a new federation, the General Confederation of Labour (CGT), which was inspired by the anarchist and Allemanist strategy of the general strike. This operated in tandem with the Federation of *Bourses du Travail*, of which Pelloutier was secretary after 1895.

Revolution or reform?

It has been debated as to whether the Paris Commune was a proletarian revolution. There is no doubt however that it was a revolution, and it gave scope in the organisation of insurrection to those professionals of revolution, the Blanquists. For a decade, the leading revolutionaries who survived were in exile. But in 1881 a number of them – Edouard Vaillant, Emile Eudes and Ernest Granger – returned to form the Central Revolutionary Committee. For publicity, they had the support of Henri Rochefort's paper, *The Intransigent* (**75**).

By 1881, however, the democratic Republic was established. Secret societies and armed uprisings seemed to be a thing of the past. Socialists were coming to accept that the best way to gain power was through the ballot box. As the parliamentary elections of 1881 approached, for example, the Guesdist Workers' Party evolved a minimum programme of reforms on which they would run, trying to draw votes from the radicals, and keeping their maximum programme up their sleeves. If he felt embarrassed about shelving revolution, Guesde could always argue that he was using the election campaign as a means of propaganda. Between 1882 and 1890, indeed, he spoke at no less than 1,200 meetings. Even the Blanquists did not exclude themselves from the electoral game. To demand an amnesty for the Communards, the aged Blanqui stood in an election at Bordeaux in 1879 (which was annulled) and again at Lyon in 1880 (in which he was defeated). Vaillant was elected to the Paris municipal council in 1884. The Boulanger episode seduced Rochefort and Blanquists like Granger, who saw the possibility of triggering off an insurrection in the popular quarters of Paris, but Vaillant came out violently against Boulanger and, fully accepting elections as the road to power, moved close to Guesde in the years after 1890.

The electoral strategy of the socialists soon paid off. In the municipal elections of May 1892 they gained a majority on 23 councils. This made it possible to find employment in town-hall administration for militants who had lost their jobs in workshops and factories. In the parliamentary elections of 1893 the socialists increased their tally from 12 to 48 seats; a 'red belt' began to take shape in the Paris suburbs (**54**) and Guesde was himself elected in the northern textile town of Roubaix. Socialists demonstrated their popularity at the polls [**doc. 8a**]. But the question still remained as to whether they were capable of transforming the bourgeois state, which they themselves called the 'Bastille of capitalism'. The bourgeoisie was ready to resort to both legal means and force to prevent any attempt by the socialists to collectivise private property. Radical municipalities, as we have seen, punished *Bourses du Travail* for going too far with political activities or strikes by withdrawing the grants they had accorded. Municipal socialism as envisaged by Paul Brousse was impossible in the centralised French state where the Conseil d'Etat or the prefects could nullify socialist measures or prohibit communes from raising loans to fund them. Little beyond free school meals, colony holidays and public baths could ever be achieved (**76**). Lastly, to contain strikes or demonstrations such as the May Day demonstrations in favour of an eight-hour day, the government was unable to rely on a sufficiently large police force, and regularly had to call out the military. On 1 May 1891, in the wool town of Fourmies, ten demonstrators were killed by troops.

There were those, mainly outside the established socialist parties, who took the view that far from always accepting the verdict of universal suffrage, the bourgeoisie would always show its claws when threatened, and that state violence would have to be met by popular violence. Anarchism, which had formerly been the basis of a mutualist and federalist socialism, now took on the character of violent outrage so often associated with that term. The anarchists who took action were not so much manual workers as petty bourgeois or *déclassé* intellectuals who were misfits in contemporary society. They avoided socialist parties because they found them to be as authoritarian and self-seeking as any other. Fanatics for individual liberty, they attacked the obvious symbols of oppression: the police, judges, deputies and soldiers (**77, 78**).

On the same day as the massacre at Fourmies, anarchists waving red flags joined May Day demonstrators at Clichy, a suburb of Paris. Shots were exchanged and arrests made. The prosecution demanded the death penalty for the three accused. In the event the maximum sentence passed was five years. But Ravachol, a common law murderer and thief who escaped to Paris, set off bombs in the apartment blocks of the judges who had sentenced the Clichy anarchists. He was executed in July 1892, brazenly abusing authority and religion at the scaffold, and at once became a popular hero. On 9 December 1893 Auguste Vaillant (not the Blanquist), who had failed to make his fortune in Argentina, threw a bomb into the Chamber of Deputies. No one was killed, but he was duly executed. A week after the execution a bomb was thrown into the Café Terminus of St Lazare Station. The perpetrator was Emile Henry, a youth of 21, son of a Communard who had fled to Spain and been condemned to death in his absence. Henry had just failed to get into the Ecole Polytechnique. He was entranced by Souvarine, the Russian anarchist of Zola's *Germinal*, and sympathised with the striking miners of Carmaux (his first bomb had been planted at the Paris offices of the Carmaux mining company). But he felt that all idle bourgeois were a legitimate target; hence his choice of a station restaurant [**doc. 8b**]. Henry was executed in May 1894. President Carnot, who had pardoned none of the anarchists, was assassinated at Lyon a month later.

Labour leaders such as Fernand Pelloutier did not approve of the bombings. On the other hand it was clear that bourgeois government, under pressure, would turn to force. The Prime Minister, Charles Dupuy, decided that the Paris *Bourse du Travail* was a hotbed of revolutionary activity, and in July 1893 sent the troops in to close it. His excuse was that the *Bourse* existed to find jobs for workers, not to strengthen the labour movement: 'It is not the unions' hotel', he told the Senate, 'it is the free labour market' (**59**, p. 87). In February and July 1894 emergency legislation – nicknamed the *lois scélérats* (villainous laws) – was passed in an attempt to gag anarchist conspiracy and propaganda, and a trial of thirty anarchists was held in August. Pelloutier argued that politics was weighted against the workers. They must plan for a revolutionary general strike which, unlike resistance on the barricades, would swamp the military, and give rise to 'the free association of free producers' [**doc. 8c**]. In 1895 he called upon surviving anarchist militants to enter trade unions and create a mass movement: anarcho-syndicalism. One of those who listened was Emile Pouget, who had been forced to leave his provincial *lycée* at the age of fifteen following the deaths of his father and stepfather, and had found a job at the Bon Marché store in Paris. Between 1889 and 1894 and after 1896 he edited a scurrilous anarchist paper, *Le Père Peinard*. However, not all trade unionists liked Pelloutier's ideas. The printers' union remained moderate. And the miners of the Pas-de-Calais – the Nottinghamshire of France – wanted to use their money not to launch strikes but to fund a deputy who would speak for them in parliament. In 1891 their leader, Basly, was elected deputy for Lens (**58**).

Class war or Jacobinism?

The Guesdists were the irreconcilable enemies of the bourgeoisie and firmly committed to the class war. This was not surprising, given the experience of the Paris Commune; and the myth of the Commune as class war was maintained by the Guesdists in their press and in their processions to the *Mur des Fédérés*, before which hundreds of Communards had been shot (**79**). The first procession, on 23 May 1880, was followed by 25,000 people. The Guesdists argued that wage-slavery had to be abolished before any other problem could be tackled. Indeed all other forms of slavery would cease once economic emancipation had come about. The workers, they insisted, were indifferent to questions relating to the constitution, or to Church and State. A socialist feminist organisation, the Union of Women, was unable to win the support of the Guesdists for the cause of women's emancipation after 1880, because the Guesdists were interested in emancipating women workers as workers first, and as women later. Indeed they saw the emancipation of women not in terms of giving them the right to work, but in terms of the freedom from want and drudgery which would allow them to stay at home as wives and mothers (**80**).

Despite this Marxist posturing, Engels noted in 1885 that 'knowledge of [Marxist] theory, even among the leaders, leaves much to be desired' (**70**, p. 30). There was in fact an in-built opposition to Marxism in France. It was regarded as German and Jewish, materialist, and of little relevance, given France's own revolutionary tradition in which socialism could be accommodated. According to this view it was pointless to deny the advantages conferred by the bourgeois revolution and the bourgeois Republic, or to ignore the Jacobin tradition which was part of the political culture of so many French workers. Rather, the socialist message must be that the Revolution of 1789 had not gone far enough: it had established political equality but not social justice. This was the goal of the proletariat, who must continue the work started by the bourgeoisie in 1789. They must convert the democratic Republic into the democratic *and social* Republic. But the Republic was the necessary framework of their crusade. Benoît Malon, a former Communard and dye-worker in Paris, took this line in the *Revue socialiste*, which he edited. In February 1889, reflecting on Boulangism, which had seduced not a few socialists, he wrote that 'the democratic and progressive Republic is the basis of our action, and we must be prepared to defend it against the reactionaries as well as against its dubious saviours'.

There were practical as well as ideological roots to Jacobinism. The electoral system was such that socialists could not always go it alone, and had to make deals with bourgeois republicans (**81**). The strength of Guesde's Workers' Party, for instance, was in large-scale industry which had a well-defined proletariat, especially in smallish single-industry towns such as Roubaix (textiles), Troyes (stocking-weaving) and Montluçon (iron founding). However in large towns with highly-differentiated populations in which the proletariat was far from being a majority, such as Lille, the Guesdists had to co-operate with the radicals in order to win the town in 1896 (**82**). The Guesdists were basically a working-class party, but it was not impossible for them to gain support in the countryside. This was easiest where class tensions were sharp, as in the Allier, where 29 per cent of the party membership in 1894–9 were *métayers* or other peasants (**83**). Communal traditions in the countryside – forest rights or the right to graze livestock on the stubble – gave some purchase to socialist missionaries, but they had to be cautious with such terms as 'collectivism', saying that they meant co-operatives or the ownership of forests by communes, not any threat to private property. In the Midi, where class tensions were more diffuse than in the north, there was a vigorous Montagnard or social-democratic tradition going back to 1849–52. This could be exploited by socialists after 1880, though they had to remember that in the South socialism meant protest, not Marxism (**84**). The Workers' Party duly supported the radical-socialist doctor, Ernest Ferroul, in his capture of the municipality of Narbonne in 1888, while in the parliamentary elections of 1898 socialist federations in the Midi (in spite of orders from Paris) sought alliances with radical-socialists from the first ballot.

In the Chamber of Deputies there were also pressures on socialists to reach agreement with bourgeois radicals. After 1893 there were fifty socialists in the Chamber, including 'independent' socialists who had been elected on another ticket and then switched to socialism. Jean Jaurès, the great socialist tribune, was originally elected for Carmaux as a radical (**85**). Millerand, a barrister elected as a radical in Paris in 1885, made his name by defending Marx's son-in-law, Paul Lafargue, who was sent for trial for provoking the tragic demonstration at Fourmies in 1891. Millerand wanted not only to reinvigorate the radical party with socialist ideas, but also to keep socialism on a legal, parliamentary tack by building a bridge from radicalism (**86**).

Socialists collaborated in the Chamber with radicals against the authoritarian measures of the government. They supported the radical ministry of Léon Bourgeois in 1895–6. After socialist success in the municipal elections of 1896, Millerand proposed a programme at St Mandé outside Paris which he hoped would unite all socialists and make way for electoral alliances with radicals in 1898. It was a very dilute programme: the acquisition of power by universal suffrage (not by revolution), the gradual transfer of private to social property and a balance between international commitment and patriotism. However, it remained to be seen how far along the road radicals – popularly described as having their hearts on the left and wallets on the right – were prepared to go. Collaboration to defend the republican form could easily give way to disagreement about content.

6   The Consolidation of the Elite

The organisation of the labour movement and socialism represented a new political menace. After 1890 it was in the interest of the French ruling class to sink its differences about religion and the constitution and organise itself in the defence of private property. The difficulty was that the republican regime – the only one among the major European states – was still contested; and the struggle to keep the republicans out of power in the 1870s had hardened the republicans in power against sharing it with anyone else. The principle of republican legitimacy and the requirements of social order were at odds with one another. Nevertheless there were attempts in the 1890s to sidestep political obstacles and construct a united ruling class on other bases.

Economic protection

World competition, falling prices for industrial goods, raw materials and foodstuffs, and declining rents and land values excited a drive for protection among agricultural and certain industrial interests. Outside parliament the Society of Agriculturalists and the Association of French Industry, which represented textiles and iron and steel, forged an alliance in 1889, with their eyes on the revision of the tariff due in 1892. The elections of October 1889 were a blow to the Right – not least to those who had flirted with Boulangism – and many conservatives now concluded that their main interest lay not in trying to change the constitution but in pooling their resources with property-owners in general and pushing for protection. The aim was not just to safeguard sales and investments, but to stabilise the countryside, reduce the rural depopulation which gave rise to unemployment and social conflict in the towns, and to organise the possessing classes in response to the organisation of the labouring classes. Two months after the elections, in December 1889, an all-party agricultural protection group formed in the Chamber of Deputies, three or four hundred strong, under the presidency of Jules Méline, who had been responsible for the tariff of 1885. A similar all-party industrial protection group was also founded.

It remained to be seen whether the protectionist alliance could be converted into political capital. In March 1890 a former Boulangist, Jacques Piou, gathered together a Constitutional Right group based on the north of France which not only favoured protection but was also prepared to accept the Republic. Unfortunately it included only sixteen deputies. The vast majority of the Right was protectionist, but saw no question of abandoning the monarchy. The most that can be said is that the tariff that went through in 1892, baptised the Méline tariff, reconciled as many of the conflicting interests of the possessing classes as possible. It was heavily but not purely protectionist, making strategic exceptions where necessary (**87**). Conservatives were induced to live within the Republican church, although they could not be brought to the altar.

The *Ralliement*

The religious question, and in particular the school question, sharply divided Catholic conservatives from republicans. The Catholic Church was seen to have supported fallen monarchies and more recently the authoritarian Empire and the Moral Order regime of 1873–7. At the same time religion could be seen as a reinforcement of the social order, and after 1890 social order was at a premium. Many republicans were prepared to admit that the lay laws were too harsh, especially in the case of the education of girls, and that the attempt to replace the catechism in state schools by a code of secular morality had been a failure. Moderate conservatives like Jacques Piou were anxious to take advantage of what might be a disaggregation of the republican camp. He particularly hated the radicals, who since 1885 had been in a position to dictate anticlerical measures to the Opportunists. But Opportunists such as Etienne Lamy were willing to relax the lay laws, and it was Piou's strategy to accept the Republic in order to displace the radicals and form a new government majority composed of Opportunists and the moderate Right (**88**).

Other conservatives were working towards this position. Albert de Mun had also played with Boulangism but his fundamental commitment was to religious and social defence. He believed that the French bourgeoisie was responsible in spite of itself for social

division and discontent: it had sown the wind of economic liberalism only to reap the whirlwind of international socialism. Christian charity was not enough to redeem the situation; the weight
of government legislation must be put behind the relief of the
working-classes. This was not purely an act of love. It would smite
atheistic revolution and help to restore the harmonious Christian
social order which de Mun believed to have existed in the Middle
Ages (**36**). De Mun's line was endorsed by Pope Leo XIII in his
encyclical of 1891, *Rerum novarum*. The Pope was also worried about
revolution. But Leo also had his own diplomatic reasons for calling
on the co-operation of the French state. The Papacy was on bad
terms with Italy since unification had absorbed the Papal States,
and since 1888 Leo had been on bad terms with Germany. He
needed the support of the French state to end his diplomatic
isolation, and therefore French Catholics must reconcile themselves
to the Republic. To test opinion Pope Leo spoke through Cardinal
Lavigerie, Archbishop of Algiers. At a banquet on 12 November
1890 Lavigerie told naval officers of the French Mediterranean
squadron that when a country was on the brink of an abyss (by
which he understood socialism) and only unreserved support for
the government of that country could save it, then that support
was necessary. He then gave a toast to the French Republic
(**89**).

This gesture was intolerable to die-hard royalists. The Republic
was unacceptable not only because it was a republic, but because
it was so incorrigibly anticlerical. The message went out from a
royalist meeting in Nîmes that even if the republican door were
opened the republicans would 'make the door so low that we would
have to get on to our stomachs to pass through it' (**89a**). It was
one thing to snub Lavigerie, another to snub the Pope. But true-
blue royalists were simply not prepared to sacrifice their royalism
to their Catholicism. Pope Leo made his views clear in his encyclical *Inter innumeras* of February 1892. He distinguished the constitution of a country, which was fixed, from its laws, which were not,
and he urged French Catholics to accept the one and strive to
change the other. Albert de Mun was happy to bow to the encyclical, and accept the Republic, but he found the doors of the
royalist salons closed in his face. Only in economically advanced
areas like the North, where social conflict was bitter and the
nobility weak, did royalists rally to the Republic as instructed (**90**).
In more backward regions such as the West and Midi, where social
conflict was less pronounced, the nobility was entrenched, and the

Republic had been resisted by counter-revolution and White Terror for a century, the *Ralliement* was a total failure.

It has been said that there were Opportunists who were willing to consider some relaxation of the lay laws and to reach some accommodation with *Ralliés* – conservatives who were prepared to accept the Republic. The moment was a good one, for the Opportunist oligarchy was under siege from former Boulangists, who were now taking up anti-Semitism as a stick with which to beat what they called the 'Jewish party'. Maurice Barrès, a young journalist, stood as an anti-Semite at Nancy in the parliamentary elections of October 1889, having calculated that anti-Semitism had electric force as a popular protest against capitalist exploitation and political manipulation (**91**). Edouard Drumont, who had published the best-selling *La France juive* in 1886, helped to found a French National Anti-Semitic League which had a former Boulangist elected to parliament in 1890. Drumont soon launched an anti-Semitic paper, *La Libre Parole*, which scored a direct hit on the Opportunist oligarchy in November 1892 with the exposure of the Panama scandal. The Panama company, thirsty for finance to build its canal, and requiring a law to authorise a share-issue, used a pair of Jewish agents – the Frankfurt banker Jacques de Reinach and Cornelius Herz – to bribe ministers and deputies in order to have the law pushed through in 1888. The exposure of these dealings set back the careers of Rouvier and Clemenceau, ruined those of Floquet and Freycinet, and ended the Opportunist golden age of 1879–93. Jacques de Reinach committed suicide (**92, 93, 94**).

France was then on the eve of elections. The discrediting of republicans in general and Opportunists in particular reopened the way to a new government majority which included *Ralliés*. The indefatigable Jacques Piou urged this course in a *Figaro* article of January 1893: the majority must include all those who were dedicated to 'an open, tolerant, and honest Republic' [**doc. 9a**]. In anticipation he renamed his Constitutional Right the Republican Right. However the new Prime Minister, Charles Dupuy, a former Education Minister and uncompromised in the Panama episode, stuck rigidly to the canon of republican legitimacy. He took four radicals into his cabinet with a view to a 'republican concentration' at the elections, and in a speech at Toulouse in May 1893 firmly rejected Piou's approach [**doc. 9b**]. Dupuy went into the elections of August–September 1893 alongside the radicals. Many *Ralliés* made their point by withdrawing at the second ballot, and instructing their followers to support a moderate republican against a socialist, but the compliment was rarely repaid by republicans. As a result the *Ralliés* lost heavily: only 36 out of 94 candidates were elected, and de Mun and Piou were among those defeated. Etienne Lamy also lost. On the other hand the radicals did well and the socialists quadrupled their tally to 48 seats.

Subduing anarchists and radicals

The main challenge to the government was now on the Left and radicals and socialists worked well together as a Jacobin opposition. Ministries were moderate in complexion, and inclined towards the Right, but an alliance with the Right was impossible: the principle of republican legitimacy established that a ministry required not just a majority but a majority of republicans.

Even before the elections, in July 1893, Dupuy clamped down by closing the *Bourse du Travail* of Paris. After the elections, in November, the socialists Millerand and Jaurès interpellated the ministry on its 'retrograde and provocative policies'. A radical minister resigned and the radicals argued that since the solidarity of the ministry was compromised it should resign as a whole. It did. The succeeding premier, Jean Casimir-Périer, grandson of the prime minister of Louis-Philippe, son of the architect of the constitution of 1875, and himself a major shareholder in the Anzin mining company, declared that his ministry wanted no revision of the constitution, no more attacks on the Church and no tax reforms which would soak the rich. One answer to this was the bomb that was thrown into the Chamber of Deputies on 9 December. The reaction of the government was determined. The *lois scélérats* passed in February and July 1894 were intended to exorcise the anarchist menace. The anarchist press was effectively muzzled, but leading militants were not included among the 30 anarchists brought to trial in August, and the prosecution failed to prove the charge of conspiracy.

Conservatives now reasoned that the time was ripe to demand more liberty for the Catholic Church. In March 1894 they pressed the Minister of Education and Ecclesiastical Affairs, Eugene Spuller, to concentrate his attack on other fanaticisms rather than to preside over such pinpricks as the refusal by the mayor of St Denis to allow religious banners in street processions. Spuller agreed that a 'new spirit' would henceforth inform government dealings with the Church. However this ignored the fact that for most republicans the Catholic Church was not simply a religion but a political force which was allied to conservatism. A deputy from the Basque country, Louis Barthou, proposed the amendment that the rights of the lay state (principally the state appointment of bishops) and 'republican' (that is, lay) education laws must remain intact. This amendment, which effectively negated the 'new spirit', was rejected by all but a few conservatives. A further attempt to build a bridge to Catholics was the bill put forward by a group of moderate republicans to nationalise the cult of Joan of Arc, who had been declared Venerable – the first step to canonisation – by the Pope in January 1894. The anniversary of the liberation of Orléans, 8 May, was to become a national holiday. There was unfortunately insufficient middle ground to secure agreement. Catholic conservatives exalted the divine, not the national, mission of Joan of Arc and insisted that she had been summoned by angels; republicans on the other hand had no time for angels and wanted to appropriate Joan as a popular heroine, who had shown up the faults of the Catholic Church, the nobility and the monarchy. The political sense of Catholicism remained an obstacle to the alliance of moderate men on both sides (**95**).

Material issues were far more likely to produce consensus. Moderate men were generally men of property and they could agree that private property had to be defended. The threat came from the radicals, supported by the socialists, and their project of a progressive income tax. A radical-based majority asserted itself in May 1894 when the Casimir-Périer government refused to allow employees of the state railways to attend a national railwaymen's congress and was overturned. The radicals were kept out of power by a succession of presidents: Carnot, who preferred Dupuy; Casimir-Périer, who succeeded briefly on Carnot's assassination, and also preferred Dupuy; and Félix Faure, who preferred Ribot. When Faure finally gave in to the radicals, it was in the same way that Grévy had finally given in to Gambetta: to let them do their worst, disgust their rivals and discredit themselves.

The cabinet formed by the radicals in November 1895 was headed by the inaptly-named Léon Bourgeois. It had the support of the socialists and a broad programme of social reform. This included further limitation of the working day, accident insurance to be paid for by employers and pensions to be paid for by both employers and employees, complete freedom of association for trade unions and the compulsory arbitration of labour disputes. In addition, the burden of taxation was to be moved from the poor to the rich by a shift from indirect to direct taxation, in particular by the introduction of a graduated income tax and inheritance tax. Bourgeois's reforms were based on an ideology of Solidarism, which was designed to correct the injustices of capitalism and persisting inequalities in the Republic. This held that there was in society a quasi-contract (that is, one recognised to exist only after it is made) whereby all members of society had a right to take from the benefits left by previous generations, and also a duty to contribute to the stock that could be enjoyed by future generations. Those who took more out of society in the form of material advantages and income than others had a debt to society which had to be repaid if class conflict were to be avoided. It was the responsibility of the government, said Bourgeois, to enforce the payments of these debts at law (**96**, **97**, **98**).

This doctrine entailed no levelling of society: once his debts had been paid the individual could make his own way in the world according to his ability. Neither was it collectivist: Bourgeois insisted that the existence of private property was a precondition of liberty. However it was not doctrine that mattered but the menace of income tax and the fact that the Bourgeois ministry was seen to be a tool of the socialists. Even with the conservatives the moderate republicans were in a minority in the Chamber. Their answer was to resort to the Senate, which twice voted no confidence in the ministry. Bourgeois riposted that he had a majority in the Chamber, and was going on. The Senate then blocked the credit of the ministry and Bourgeois was obliged to resign.

The cabinet of Jules Méline which now took office was one of the longest-lasting before the war, in power from April 1896 until May 1898. It was a moderate republican ministry which survived with the votes of the Right, which was strictly against the rules of republican legitimacy. Radicals and socialists immediately challenged it on the grounds that it had a majority of republicans against it. The significant thing is that Méline did not deny the importance of the rules. Speaking in October 1897 he tried to turn them to his advantage. He argued that without the socialists the radicals would themselves be in a republican minority (and by implication that socialists were as un-republican as the Right). Moreover he concentrated on the question of measures, not men. The ministry did not intend to declare war on religion, he said, but he underlined that 'our policy is republican, clearly republican' [**doc. 10**]. Republicans drew their own conclusions from the obvious relaxation of the lay laws under the ministry and Méline's symbolic attendance at Notre-Dame for the memorial service for the victims of a fire at a large Paris department store.

The restoration of French greatness

The Republic as a regime at home was much more contested than the Republic as a power abroad. There were Catholics who believed that the conversion of Clovis on the battlefield of Tolbiac gave France her identity as 'the eldest daughter of the Church', and that Catholics should regard Rome as their fatherland as much as France. But France as a colonial power, establishing hegemony over Muslims, Buddhists and animists, was a Christian and Catholic power, engaged in a civilising mission. The Republic and the Church went hand in hand. In Gambetta's famous phrase, anticlericalism was not for export. One of the most influential figures in France's colonial expansion was indeed Lavigerie, the Archbishop of Algiers, capital of her oldest colony. His appointment as papal administrator of Carthage and Tunis in 1881, which gave him jurisdiction over the Italian clergy there, was crucial in France's establishment of a protectorate in Tunis in defiance of Italian claims. As papal delegate for the Sahara and Sudan he sent out his missionaries, the White Fathers, to create new sees in Equatorial Africa and lay the foundations of French power. It is no accident that he was chosen in 1890 to urge French Catholics to accept the Republic whose interests he had done so much to further (**99**).

A second factor which induced many conservatives to look favourably on the Republic was the Franco-Russian alliance, sealed by military and diplomatic conventions in 1891 and 1892. Under these Russia agreed to support France if she were attacked by Germany; on the other hand France was not bound to support Russia in the Dardanelles in any conflict Russia had with Great Britain (which would have been rather different from the Crimean War). The Republic felt secure for the first time in a generation: its isolation, both diplomatic and constitutional in a Europe of monarchies, was ended. This was symbolised by the visit of a French naval squadron to the Russian base of Kronstadt in July 1891, when the arch-reactionary Tsar, Alexander III, stood bareheaded to a rendering of the *Marseillaise*. The alliance was reinforced by the visit of Tsar Nicholas II and the Tsarina Alexandra to France in October 1896 and the return visit of President Faure to Russia a year later. These were some of the earliest public events caught on film, and the success of them was so great that for a time Méline considered the step (unprecedented since 1877) of holding elections before the Chamber had run its full term.

Rivalry with Great Britain in the colonial sphere was a third factor which induced loyalty to the Republic (**100**). Relations had been bad since Anglo-French condominion in Egypt had given way to British military occupation in 1882. An agreement of August 1890 settling a number of African questions was widely considered to be to France's disadvantage. To protest against this and to pursue the goal of French greatness in Africa, a Committee of French Africa was set up. It was headed by the Prince d'Arenberg, the president of the Suez Canal company. Since d'Arenberg was a member of Piou's Constitutional Right and the Committee also included republicans, there was evidence of all-party collaboration on a colonial issue. This was deepened with the formation of an all-party Colonial Group in the Chamber which numbered 90 deputies before the elections of 1893 and 120 afterwards. It was formed mainly of moderates from the republican and conservative sides, and had the active support of Eugène.Étienne, the republican deputy for Oran and Under-Secretary of State for Colonies (**101**). These pressure groups sharpened their teeth on colonial conflicts with Great Britain. In 1896 the French army put down a revolt in the protectorate of Madagascar and turned it into a colony, but the British had long been influential with the native ruling house, especially through Methodist missionaries, and were accused of fomenting the rebellion. This provoked much popular anti-British and anti-Protestant feeling in France. The long-term plan of the Committee of French Africa was to cut the route Great Britain seemed to be making from the Cape to Cairo by seizing control of the Upper Nile and trying to displace her from Egypt. To this effect an expedition left France in June 1896 under Captain Jean-Baptiste Marchand. As things turned out, however, it was to contribute little to French greatness and something, indirectly, to French domestic instability (**102**).

7 The Dreyfus Affair

That the court martial of a Jewish army officer could churn French life into a foam of passion for the best part of five years and in some way generate the currents that would inform all French politics and intellectual controversy in the twentieth century is one of the paradoxes of the Third Republic (**103, 104, 105**). Part of the explanation lies in France's continuing sense of insecurity and her eagerness to find scapegoats for her military setbacks. Part of it is to be found in an eruption of anti-Semitism at the end of the nineteenth century, less virulent than the strains found in Germany, Austria and Russia, but remarkable in a country which had a population of only 80,000 Jews, 0.2 per cent of the total population. This irrational feeling provoked the intervention of intellectuals, who believed that the Jewish captain had been condemned either unjustly or irregularly; in fact the Affair was one of intellectuals – writers, teachers, students and journalists – far more than it was one of politicians. In opposition to these intellectuals there sprang up a new Right which was characterised less by royalism (though royalism was far from dead) than by a nationalism that saw France being torn apart by non-French elements. After the interlude of the 1890s, when some rapprochement between republicans and conservatives had at least been attempted, the Dreyfus Affair scored even more deeply the line dividing republicans from non-republicans. This was because the 'non-French' elements attacked by the nationalists were none other than the republicans who had run France for the last twenty years, while the republicans were forced to close ranks to defend the Republic in danger and their monopoly of political power.

Anti-Semitism

'The anti-Semites do not know the Jews,' wrote Charles Péguy in 1910; 'they talk about them, but they do not know them at all' (**105a**). Anti-Semitism said more about anti-Semites than it did about Jews. Bernard-Lazare, an anarchist of Jewish origins, argued

51

that 'anti-Semitism is a capitalist trick to safeguard the totality of the banking, industrial and landowning class by a small and cleverly limited operation. Capital would have its Jewish foreskin circumcised in order to function with greater security' (**105b**). The idea was to deflect working-class and socialist anger on to one section of capitalists to secure the rest. Hence the epithet: 'the socialism of fools'. Anti-Semitism was also a means of bringing the French masses back to the Catholic Church by attacking the Jews for killing Christ and for pursuing a mission of dechristianisation in the Third Republic, including divorce and the state secondary education of women. Jews had indeed been behind these two measures; but if it had been pointed out that Ferry was not Jewish, the anti-Semites would have replied that Ferry was married to a Protestant, and that Protestants were half Jewish. Lastly, anti-Semitism was a means to prop up French greatness by blaming defeat and humiliation on Jews who, even though they had been given French citizenship in 1791, remained for the anti-Semites unassimilated, cosmopolitan, the treacherous agents of a world conspiracy, in short, the true heirs of Judas (**94**). Drumont's *Libre Parole* attacked Jewish army officers from its inception in 1892. Captain Alfred Dreyfus, who was court-martialled in 1894 and sent for life to Devil's Island for selling military secrets to the Germans, served only to confirm the myth of the Jewish traitor. 'That Dreyfus is capable of treachery', wrote Barrès in 1899, 'I conclude from his race' (**105c**).

There was, however, a small knot of faithful who believed that Dreyfus had not betrayed France and had indeed been framed by certain officers of the general staff. Lieutenant-Colonel Picquart, who took over the Intelligence Section in 1895 and began to suspect irregularities, was hurried off to Tunisia by his superiors. At the end of 1896 Bernard-Lazare published in Brussels a pamphlet entitled, *A Judicial Error: the Truth about the Dreyfus Affair*. Jews such as Bernard-Lazare, Dreyfus's brother Matthieu, and Joseph Reinach (the nephew and son-in-law of Jacques) were at the forefront of the campaign to reopen the case, and were easily denounced as agents of an international Jewish 'syndicate' which intended to discredit the army and ruin France. But they were involved as individuals. The Jews as a community showed no solidarity with Dreyfus; rather they kept their heads down, hoping that the problem would go away (**106**).

Intellectuals

If the Jewish Dreyfusards belonged to a group, it was to the intellectuals. It was the intellectuals who *created* the Affair (**107**, **108**, **109**). First, they revolutionised the presentation of what was happening. They believed that such fetishisms as the honour of the army, *raison d'Etat*, and racism lay behind the condemnation of Dreyfus and its popular acceptance. They were convinced equally that a scientific examination of the facts would reveal the innocence of Dreyfus and the pernicious role of highly-placed officers, even the former Minister of War, General Mercier [**doc. 11**]. The acquittal by the military of the man they suspected, Major Esterhazy, in January 1898, acted as a starting-gun for them. Second, the intellectuals were conscious of belonging to a very small group. They were defined as intellectuals against manual workers and politicians and also against the mass of the population which was seduced by appearances and motivated by prejudice rather than reason. The intellectuals were isolated and persecuted, but drew strength from *camaraderie* and commitment to the cause.

Emile Zola was not the first to make his mark, but his open letter to the President of the Republic under the headline *J'accuse*, published in Clemenceau's paper *L'Aurore* on 13 January 1898, transformed the Affair [**doc. 12**]. He projected a technical wrangle about evidence as a drama pitting a single individual against the military establishment, Good against Evil, Light against Darkness. 'Poets', he said, 'are in some way visionaries.' He wanted to join the band which was assembling from the four corners of the horizon at 'the crossroads of truth'. His was a mission to unmask the monsters who had sent Dreyfus to Devil's Island, and his letter was 'a revolutionary means to hasten the explosion of truth and justice'. Zola's attack on named army officers was interpreted as libel. He was sent for trial, fined 3,000 francs and sentenced to a year's imprisonment. He fled to London, a martyr to the cause. 'Whoever suffers for truth and justice,' he consoled himself, 'becomes august and sacred'(**109a**).

The day after Zola's *J'accuse*, there appeared in the press a *Manifesto of the Intellectuals*. Its signatories included the young writer Marcel Proust and the more established Anatole France, who was a member of the Académie Française. France was writing a series of pieces in the *Echo de Paris* which exposed with the sharp knife of irony the hollowness and hypocrisy of the generals, clergy, nobles and converted Jews who denounced Jewish conspiracy, but he was more sceptical than Zola about the inevitable triumph of justice and truth. 'Peoples, sir,' says one of his characters, 'live on mythology' (**109b**). The intellectuals took up their positions at various vantage points. One of these was the offices of the literary and artistic *Revue blanche*. Another was the Bellais bookshop, set up in the Latin Quarter by a graduate of the Ecole Normale Supérieure, Charles Péguy. Attacked in the press of his native Orléans for his Dreyfusism and socialism, Péguy declared that 'socialism is the recovery of universal justice, while Dreyfusism is the recovery of a particular justice' (**109c**). The librarian of the Ecole Normale Supérieure, Lucien Herr, was a man of great conviction who recruited many young Normaliens to the cause (**110**). Some, like Blum and Péguy, were also inspired by his socialism. The Ecole was more Dreyfusard than socialist, but even as such it was far from being representative of students as a whole. Zola's letter to French youth of December 1897 indeed reproached it for being nationalist and anti-Semitic. Students committed to reopening the Dreyfus case could expect to be beaten up for their pains. The League of Rights of Man, set up during Zola's trial in February 1898 to defend individual rights against militarism, clericalism and nationalism, was another meeting-point of Dreyfusard intellectuals. It included both Freemasons like Ludovic Trarieux and (at first) the liberal Catholic Paul Viollet. However, it remained rather a small organisation until the summer of 1898 (**111**).

Politicians

Politicians reacted in a very different way from intellectuals. They could not deal with truth and falsehood in an abstract sense but had to take public opinion into account. In particular they wanted to be sure of their re-election to parliament, and elections were due in May 1898. Anti-Semitism was a force which any politician ignored at his peril. Zola's trial was greeted by anti-Semitic riots in eastern France (where there were some Jews) and in western France (where there were none). In Algeria, which had a Jewish population of 30,000, there were pogroms. The French Anti-Semitic League was revived in 1897 by a bankrupt oil-refiner, Jules Guérin, with publicity provided by *La Libre Parole*, and campaigned to get Drumont elected at Algiers. Drumont was successful, as were twenty-one other professed anti-Semites, in the elections of 1898 (**93**, **94**). An analysis of the press in the run-up to the elections shows that only seven of the fifty-five major dailies, six of them

Parisian, were Dreyfusard (**112**). Clemenceau, editor of *L'Aurore*, was behaving more like an intellectual than a politician. He had lost his seat as a result of the Panama scandal and was happy in his old role of savaging parliament and ministers. Most of the press either argued that the interests of order, the country and the army had to be put before the interest of an individual, or was blatantly anti-Dreyfusard and anti-Semitic.

It was not that the Left was for Dreyfus and the Right against. There was a plebeian, anti-capitalist, left-wing anti-Semitism which the socialist leaders had to confront. Only the anarchists and Allemanists, including Pelloutier and Péguy, were resolutely 'Dreyfusards of the first hour'. This derived from their moralism and their fierce antimilitarism and anticlericalism, but also from the fact that as anarchists they were not seeking election to parliament. Parliamentary socialist leaders were much more prudent. Millerand was deaf to the blandishments of Péguy. Guesde said that Zola's letter was the greatest revolutionary act of the century, but refused to let the working class become involved in a bourgeois civil war which obscured their ultimate goal of collectivism. Jaurès was torn between his intellectual background as a Normalien and academic and his commitment to the masses, which caused him to suspect the Opportunists and Panamists among the Dreyfusards, and to put the unity of the socialist movement before all else. Those who hesitated were lost. Both Jaurès and Guesde lost their seats in the elections of May 1898. Only after the elections did the political landscape change. Jaurès in the wilderness tried to unite the socialists behind the Dreyfusard cause. His perspective on the Affair was now purely Jacobin. 'Since Reaction has formed a bloc,' he told a rally in June, 'the Revolution must form a bloc' (**85**). However Guesde feared that Jaurès would run off with the socialist party and refused to follow. The proletariat, he announced, would not tie itself to the tail of 'the bourgeoisie of the prisons and firing squads of 1871'. It was not until the government sent in 60,000 troops to break a railwaymen's strike in October 1898 that Guesde agreed to align his party with Jaurès and the Dreyfusard front. For a brief moment an alliance of workers and intellectuals had been achieved.

The radicals hated Jules Méline who had displaced them in 1896 and who denied that there was a Dreyfus Affair. But they did not for all that take up the cause of Dreyfus, either before or after the elections of May 1898, which returned them to power. They were much happier attacking the Church than the army. Godefroy

Cavaignac, the War Minister in the radical cabinet of Henri Brisson, went so far as to stand up in the Chamber on 9 July 1898 to say that he had irrefutable proof of the guilt of Dreyfus. Jaurès, in an article he published the following month, demonstrated that this 'proof' was a fake produced by an officer in the Intelligence Section, Colonel Henry. Henry confessed to Cavaignac, was duly arrested and slit his throat in prison. More inclined to sympathy with Dreyfus were the moderate republicans, those in the Senate even more than those in the Chamber. The vice-president of the Senate, Auguste Scheurer-Kestner, a Protestant from Alsace, was one of the first and most influential Dreyfusards. Other Protestants and freemasons followed his lead. Many moderates were best described as revisionists: they were persuaded less of Dreyfus's innocence than of the irregularities of military justice in the matter, and therefore pressed for the case to be reopened. Perhaps, as Ferry had said, the Senate was the fortress of the Republic.

Nationalism

The suicide of Colonel Henry acted as a catalyst. For the Dreyfusards the military had condemned itself by its own hand and the case for revision was unanswerable. But when certain members of the government, such as the Foreign Minister, Delcassé, began to admit the case for revision, the anti-Dreyfusards hit back, whipping up nationalist sentiment. Domestic politics and foreign affairs became inseparable. Cavaignac and the War Minister who followed him resigned rather than be a party to revision. The government was attacked by the nationalists not only for wavering over Dreyfus, but also for failing to stand up to the British. For at that moment Kitchener, having made his way up the Nile, arrived with far superior numbers at Fashoda, where Captain Marchand had established his base. Delcassé, who was concerned about a possible confrontation with the British navy, wanted a negotiated peace, and offered to recall Marchand. This was discovered by the nationalist press, and a massive demonstration in protest on 28 October 1898 overturned the Brisson government. Delcassé however remained Foreign Minister in the next (Dupuy) government which, in the face of the mobilisation of the British navy in the Mediterranean, recalled Marchand (**113**).

The nationalist press was reluctant to see the débâcle in terms of military power. Marchand told it that he had obeyed the order to withdraw after Kitchener had sent him a bundle of French newspapers which related the course of the Affair. He said that he was not inclined to defend a putrid France which, by reopening the Dreyfus case, demonstrated its preference for Jewish traitors over and above the honour of the army. This gave fuel to the opponents of the parliamentary Republic who could argue that it was run by the enemy within who betrayed it to the enemy without [**doc. 13**]. The nationalist opposition was composed of diverse elements. First there were the royalists who detested the strategy of *Ralliement* which required them either to vote for moderate republicans or to abstain. They wanted to return to intransigence, have done with parliamentary compromise, and mobilise popular support. The *Jeunesses Royalistes* were at the forefront of this movement, but it had the support of the pretender, the Duc d'Orléans, who tried to acquire a popular arm by subsidising Jules Guérin's Anti-Semitic League and was introduced to the flower of its street-fighters, the butchers of La Villette. A second element was the *Ligue des Patriotes*, which was revived at the end of 1898 by Paul Déroulède (**33**). Déroulède was a staunch republican who aspired to a plebiscitary Republic which would be responsive to the popular will. On the other hand there was a strong Bonapartist instinct among the former NCOs and petty bourgeois who made up the League together with an amenability to the anti-Semitism of Guérin. A third element was the *Ligue de la Patrie Française*. This was founded in January 1899 by some second-rate school-masters who then brought in mandarins of the Académie Française such as François Coppée and Jules Lemaître to prove that the Dreyfusards did not have a monopoly of intellectuals. However its somewhat patrician air and rather woolly philosophy of nationalism (Barrès delivered a lecture to it on 'La Terre et les Morts' soon after its foundation) was little to the taste of younger men of extremism and action. These broke away around their own review, the *Action Française*, in July 1899 and planned to raise support in the streets (**114**).

What the nationalists had in common was their passionate opposition to the revision of the Dreyfus verdict. The 'republican aristocracy' of the Senate were, however, moving in this direction. On the death of President Félix Faure the Senate helped to elect Emile Loubet, who was understood to favour revision. Déroulède decided to pre-empt the issue by staging a *coup d'état* at the funeral of President Faure on 23 February 1899. He grasped the bridle of the horse of one of the generals and tried to persuade him to occupy the Elysée Palace – without success. Déroulède later complained that the royalists had refused their co-operation because of his declared republicanism (**115**). The final decision about whether the Dreyfus case should be sent back to the military court lay with the Appeal Court. On 3 June 1899 the Appeal Court ruled that it should. The next day, at the racecourse of Auteuil, President Loubet was set upon by nationalist demonstrators and had his hat knocked off. The cry went up that the Republic was in danger.

From *mystique* to *politique*

A ministry of republican defence came into office on 22 June under the presidency of René Waldeck-Rousseau. It looked like a classic Jacobin alliance, stretching from moderate republicans through radicals to socialists. On closer inspection it was slightly less convincing. Waldeck was a Progressist, that is, one of the republican supporters of Méline. Some of the Progressists followed Waldeck, while others stayed with Méline and drifted into the conservative camp. In spite of their name, Progressists were very moderate. The cabinet included only one radical; the slogan of republican defence was used by Brisson to mobilise reluctant radical support for the ministry. The socialist Millerand was given the Ministry of Commerce, but this did not elicit the support of Guesde, Vaillant and their followers. These marked their distance by shouting 'Vive la Commune', when the new War Minister, General Gallifet, who had helped to suppress it, took his seat in the Chamber, and by announcing on 14 July that they were returning to 'the class and therefore revolutionary policy of the militant proletariat and socialist party' (**70**, pp 423–4).

The Waldeck-Rousseau ministry presided over the liquidation of the Affair. The second court-martial of Dreyfus opened at Rennes, under the eyes of the nation, in August 1899. An acquittal would have been dangerous, given the state of agitation among the nationalists. An acquittal also ran the risk that members of the general staff and the former War Minister General Mercier might be threatened with trial, and be tempted to launch a *coup d'état* (**116**). However on 9 September Dreyfus was once more found guilty by a majority of the judges, albeit with the ridiculous qualification of 'extenuating circumstances'. Ten days later Dreyfus received a pardon from the President of the Republic. This was probably the most politic outcome for which Waldeck could have wished. But the Dreyfusards were infuriated. The clear acquittal which would have resolved the struggle between Good and Evil,

Light and Darkness, was not offered to them. Their anger was deflected by the government on to the extreme nationalists, Déroulède and Guérin, who were made into examples (accused of plotting against state security, taken before the High Court, smeared with royalist connections and sentenced respectively to six years' exile and ten years' imprisonment) and on to the Catholic Church, in particular the Assumptionists who published the anti-Semitic *La Croix* and were dissolved. By contrast the military men under suspicion were amnestied. As Zola put it, the virtuous and the rascals were put into the same bag.

The liquidation of the Affair revealed a shift between what Péguy called *mystique* and *politique*. The sense of mission of the first Dreyfusards gave way to the calculations of parties and the accommodation of interests. Dreyfusism became part of republican legitimacy, although as Péguy pointed out, those who laid claim to the mantle of Dreyfus in 1903 were just as likely to have been anti-Dreyfusard in 1898. When Péguy espoused Catholicism in 1910 with his *Mystery of the Charity of Joan of Arc*, the Catholic conservatives toasted his conversion to the Right. But, he insisted in *Notre Jeunesse*, published a few months later, Catholicism as a religion had nothing to do with Catholicism as a political position. At the beginning of the Affair, he argued, it had been possible, at the level of *mystique*, to be republican and Christian and even Jewish at the same time, for what had Dreyfusism been if not 'a religion of temporal salvation'? A 'Republic of Dreyfusards' was now in power but it represented the revenge of the politicians who had never demonstrated any of the generous commitment of the Dreyfusards of the first hour. They politicised the Affair and turned its cause into a familiar intolerant anticlericalism.

8 Radicalism

What radicalism?

Radicalism was at once the most characteristic political force in France between 1898 and 1914 and the most difficult to define. A book published by Madeleine Rebérioux in 1975 is entitled *La République radicale?*, complete with question mark (**3**). This is not unreasonable. It is open to debate whether the Radicals held power in this period, whether they constituted a proper political party and whether their policies were indeed radical.

If we look at personalities it is possible to distinguish 'old' radicals and 'new' radicals. Some radicals of a chauvinist bent, like Déroulède and Rochefort, moved across the political spectrum to the nationalist Right; what remained constant was their hatred of parliamentary oligarchy. Others, like Millerand and Jaurès, who wished for a more 'social' Republic, moved in the direction of socialism. Radicals who achieved power before the Boulanger Affair, including Floquet and Goblet, were phased out by the Panama scandal and the passage of time. The 'new' radicals came to prominence in the wake of Panama, and included Bourgeois and Brisson, who became prime ministers respectively in 1895 and 1898. They might be described as more calculating and less passionate, more realistic and less romantic. Clemenceau is not easy to classify. His career spans the whole Third Republic but it was interrupted by Panama and did not really bear fruit again until 1906, when he formed a government. Moreover, though he was in the popular view the quintessential radical, he was not a member of the Radical party except in the year 1909.

This introduces a second distinction, between radicalism as a movement and the Radical party. In a country where universal suffrage was so long established, it is perhaps surprising that organised mass parties took so long to evolve. It took the Dreyfus Affair, and the consequent agitation of opinion and raising of stakes, to provoke the organisation of parties with a recognisable discipline and ideology, and even then the congeries of self-interested groups was not far beneath the surface. The approaching elections of 1902 had a galvanising effect. Among the radicals the initiative came less from the parliamentary politicians than from the constituents. A congress held in June 1901 brought together in Paris representatives from hundreds of masonic lodges, secularist societies, provincial newspapers, constituency committees and municipalities as well as deputies and senators. This resulted in the election of an executive committee of party militants together with local councillors, deputies and senators, and the formulation of a rather vague policy commitment to 'lay, democratic and social action' [**doc. 14a**]. The wide spectrum of opinion in the party was clear even in its title, the 'Republican, Radical and Radical-Socialist Party' (**117, 118, 119**).

Other groups of politicians saw the need to follow suit. In the same month former *Ralliés* around Albert de Mun and Jacques Piou set up a Liberal Action party, which hoped to build bridges towards non-Radical republicans (**120**). These fell into two groups, which came to call themselves parties, but lacked any real constituency organisation. The first, launched in October 1901, was the Democratic Alliance, which represented the right wing of Waldeck's coalition, and was closely linked to the world of finance, industry, colonial affairs and the big daily newspapers. It included Louis Barthou, Raymond Poincaré, Maurice Rouvier, Eugène Etienne and Joseph Caillaux. The second, formed in 1903, was the Republican Federation, which represented that element of the Progressists which had followed Méline rather than Waldeck, and was not part of the ministerial coalition. It included landowners and feudal industrialists such as Eugène Motte, the textile magnate of Roubaix who had defeated Guesde in 1898.

The socialists had been the first to set up party organisations, but it still proved impossible to hold together a single socialist party. The inclusion of a socialist minister, Millerand, in the ministerial coalition provoked crisis at the first congress of socialist organisations held in Paris in December 1899 to establish a French Socialist Party. Jaurès defended ministerial participation as the natural consequence of participation in municipalities and parliament. But this was rejected by Guesde's insistence on revolutionary action and class war, which was given credibility when troops fired on striking miners at Châlon-sur-Saône in June 1900. At the second congress in September 1900 the split was wide open. Guesde formed his own Socialist Party of France, while Jaurès called imminent social revolution a hallucination. In a democracy, he said, power must be won legally by a majority, not by a revolutionary minority. The Republic was not necessarily bourgeois; it was an instrument of social justice and the 'political form of socialism'. He summed up, 'the Republic is incomplete without socialism, but socialism is powerless without the Republic' (**121**).

The Radicals, like the followers of Jaurès, were tied into the Waldeck-Rousseau coalition by the ideology of republican defence. The Radicals subscribed to the principles of the Revolution of 1789, but were far less certain about revolution in their own time. In particular they upheld the sanctity of private property which was dear, they argued, not only for its own sake, but as the condition of individual liberty. Jaurès pointed out in vain that even in the essentially bourgeois Civil Code there were restrictions on private property, such as state intervention to tax, to regulate inheritance and to expropriate for public utility, as in the case of railways. The proponents of social reform under the Waldeck-Rousseau ministry were not the Radicals but the socialist Millerand and the moderate Caillaux. Millerand as Minister of Commerce extended the ten-hour limit on the working day imposed on female workshops (1892) to mixed workshops (1900), and saw through an Associations law which enabled trade unions to hold property collectively (July 1901). Joseph Caillaux, the son of a minister who had held office as a result of the 16 May *coup* and anxious to establish his republican credentials as a young Finance Minister, cut indirect taxes on sugar and alcohol and introduced the progressive principle in his reform of death duties. However the Chamber of Deputies and not least the Radical party fought shy of too much state intervention. After all, the main constituents of the Radical party were those *classes moyennes* whose livelihoods derived from their private property – farms, small businesses or savings. Neither Caillaux's plans for progressive income tax nor Millerand's plans for pensions made any headway.

Radicals were much happier with the doctrine of anticlericalism. It served to separate Left from Right and at the same time bound together the Jacobin coalition. Even the Democratic Alliance described itself as 'anticlerical but not anti-religious'. Socialists who travelled with them were obliged to subordinate divisive issues of social reform to the immediate question, which was the defence of the Republic. The Associations law was less significant as a trade-union law than as a way of dissolving religious congregations (and the private schools they ran) on the grounds that they were not properly authorised under Napoleonic legislation. The Right changed its game accordingly. Defending the Catholic Church was worth more votes than casting doubts on the constitution. It appropriated the term liberal – as in the case of Liberal Action – claiming to protect the liberty of believers against persecution by sectarians, and it attempted to build a bridge towards moderate republicans. Because the anticlerical battle put on to ice battles over class or the constitution, it can be seen paradoxically as a stabilising force in French politics.

The *Bloc des Gauches*

Although the Right tried to gain republican respectability, the struggle over the Church tended to roll anticlericals and defenders of the Republic into one, and gave victory to the Left in the parliamentary elections of April–May 1902. The Right with 264 seats was confined to the North, North-East and West. On the government side (321 seats) there was a marked shift from moderates to Radicals, which provoked the resignation of Waldeck from the premiership. The Radicals had lost Paris to the Right in 1900, but were now as strong in the countryside as in the towns, calling themselves simply 'radical' in the North of France, and 'radical-socialist' in the South. Among the socialists the supporters of Jaurès and republican defence did much better than Guesde and the revolutionaries.

Waldeck was succeeded as premier by Emile Combes, a country doctor from the South-West, the Radical leader in the Senate. He headed a coalition called the *Bloc des Gauches*, which was steered by a committee including Jaurès and had an ample social programme, but which also had to accommodate moderates like the banker Maurice Rouvier, and therefore dedicated itself to anticlericalism (**122, 123**). This was tactically rational, but it would be unwise to underestimate the force of anticlericalism as a political passion, either in the case of Combes, who had once taught in the Assumptionist College of Nîmes, or in that of the Radical grassroots. They wanted to destroy the influence of the Catholic Church in politics and education once and for all. Combes's majority enabled him to have the Chamber reject in three short bills the requests for authorisation submitted by the religious congregations. But in the country a good deal of resistance was manifest. *Gendarmes* and even troops were sent in where necessary to clear the schoolhouses of teaching brothers, nuns and demonstrators. Albert de Mun tried to channel this ground swell

63

of Catholic opinion by refounding his party as the Popular Liberal Action. More serious were the cracks which appeared in the *Bloc des Gauches*. Waldeck-Rousseau did not approve of the dissolution of overseas missions and female teaching congregations and made things very difficult for Combes in the Senate. As a republican who had cut his political teeth in Brittany, Waldeck understood the need to court republican opinion that was also Catholic, whereas for the southerner Combes Catholicism was counter-revolution and had to be rooted out.

At the other end of the coalition, socialist leaders were worried that the anticlerical crusade was weakening their grip on the working class. However the sharpening of class conflict was beginning to reveal the true colours of the ruling Radical party. When a general miners' strike threatened in October 1902, Combes sent in the military and one miner was killed in the Loire. Anarchists like Pouget and Blanquists like the shoemaker Griffuelhes rose to power in the CGT, making possible the union of the CGT and the Federation of *Bourses du Travail* in 1902 and the defeat of moderate unions led by the printers at the Bourges congress of the CGT in September 1904. From now on the CGT was committed to a general strike for an eight-hour day, which was seen by the militants as a consciousness-raiser for a revolutionary general strike. Socialist leaders moved with the current, willingly or unwillingly. Millerand interpellated the Combes ministry in March 1904 for ignoring social reform [**doc. 14b**]. At the Amsterdam meeting of the Socialist International in August 1904, Jaurès was defeated by motions sponsored by the German Social Democrats in favour of revolutionary action and the class struggle. As a result he had to leave the *Bloc des Gauches* and defer to Guesde in a united socialist party, the French Section of the Workers' International (SFIO). The Combes ministry fell in November 1905, and was replaced by one headed by Rouvier. One last anticlerical card was played in an attempt to keep the socialists in line. The socialists had long wanted the Separation of Church and State — the termination of government subsidies to the Church and, in turn, of government powers, including the appointment of bishops. Combes had refused to countenance any relaxation of government control over the Church, but the price of socialist support was now Separation, and this was seen through by Aristide Briand, who chaired the parliamentary commission on the Separation. The bill was passed in December 1905 and Catholic opposition brushed aside. But that did not mean that the socialists were happy. For social strife was now reaching a pitch that the clarion calls of anti-clericalism could not hope to drown.

Class war

1906 was the worst year for strikes before 1936, which in turn was the worst before 1968 (**56**, **124**). They were spontaneous and violent, in response to the rising cost of living and at the fringe of a wave of strikes whose epicentre was Russia. Following the pit disaster at Courrières in the Pas-de-Calais in which 1,100 miners died, a CGT-affiliated 'young' union broke away from the 'old' union of the miners' deputy, Basly, and brought 40,000 men out on strike. The government replied by pouring 20,000 troops into the northern coalfield (**125**). At Hennebont in Brittany metallurgical workers who went on strike for 116 days in the spring and summer of 1906 were reduced to eating crabs from the beach. When Post Office workers stopped work, the government sacked 500 of them in an attempt to halt the unionisation of public employees. The CGT launched a general strike for an eight-hour day on 1 May 1906. This was opposed by the Guesdists, who, though revolutionary, wanted workers to defer to the leadership of the party and confine themselves to voting in the elections of 6 May. But 200,000 workers responded to the strike call. In Paris many of the bourgeoisie feared another Commune and started to leave. Clemenceau, then Minister of the Interior, declared a state of siege, sent in troops and arrested CGT leaders, declaring, 'Your means of action is disorder, my duty is to ensure order' (**126**).

In October 1906 Clemenceau became premier. He included in his cabinet two former socialists, Briand and Viviani, the latter at a newly-created Ministry of Labour. But there was no sign that class conflict was easing. The CGT met in congress at Amiens that same month and gave itself over to healing the divisions between reformists (led by the printers), Guesdists (strong in the textile unions) and anarcho-syndicalists. The congress accepted the need for both day-to-day work, to improve wages and conditions, and the future work of total emancipation; it also permitted the political activity of trade unionists as individuals, while asserting the political neutrality of the CGT corporately, and its commitment to direct action. At its congress at Limoges in November 1906, the SFIO accepted that the party and the union should act in parallel and in concert. These negotiations did no more than endorse the attitude of the average militant, like Pierre Soulageon of St

Etienne, who reasoned, 'I am a trade unionist at the Bourse and a socialist at the party' (**126a**). But they suspended internecine struggles over political or direct action, reform or revolution, and confronted the government with a united working class.

Strife continued for another two years. Sectors and regions not previously involved in strikes and unionisation were mobilised. In the recently mechanised boot and shoe industry there was a strike of 103 days at Fougères in Brittany in the winter of 1906–7 and another at Raon l'Etape in the Vosges where two workers were killed. Primary school teachers formed unions after 1904, gathered in a national federation in 1905 and demanded the right to affiliate to *Bourses du Travail* and the CGT. This was refused by the government in 1907 and recalcitrant teachers were dismissed. Along the Mediterranean coast winegrowers rose in revolt in the summer of 1907 against the government's failure to regulate over-production and fraud. Troops fired on demonstrators at Narbonne and Montpellier, but at Béziers they refused to fire and mutinied (**127**, **128**). The sand-quarriers of the Seine struck with the help of more skilled building workers in May 1.908. The employers brought in blacklegs who were seized by the strikers. The *gendarmes* released the blacklegs, killing two strikers in the process. Tension between the government and the labour movement reached a pitch [**doc. 15**]. The builders' union with the support of the CGT called a one-day protest strike and demonstration on 30 July. This was charged by troops, leaving another two dead. Clemenceau arrested and imprisoned the CGT leaders and would have banned the CGT but for the intervention of Viviani and Briand (**129**). A general strike called by the CGT was a failure, and this marked a turning point in the strike movement. Basly's miners' union joined the CGT in June 1908, which reinforced its moderate wing. The revolutionary secretary of the CGT, Griffuelhes, was replaced in 1909 by Léon Jouhaux, while in the SFIO influence was passing from Guesde to Jaurès. Both Jouhaux and Guesde put organisation and unity before ideological purity (**130**).

Radicals between Revolution and revolution

After the Separation of Church and State, the Radicals were in search of a programme. The advantage of anticlericalism was that it could hold together the loose alliance that was the Radical party, stretching from moderates who were more republican than radical to those whose radical-socialism was a serious commitment. Now that anticlericalism as the basis of policy had shot its bolt, the Radicals were required to define what they stood for. The programme presented to the Nancy congress of the Radical party in 1907 was full of the rhetoric of universal suffrage, belonging to the Left, and dedication to principles of the French Revolution. The vagueness was intentional, for firm proposals of social reform would immediately divide those who put ideals before wealth from those who put wealth before ideals. The question of Revolution was itself difficult. The social disorder which prevailed in France after 1906 pushed Radicals towards the Centre, but their doctrine kept them on the Left. Revolution was a legitimating principle, the cult of those who were entitled to hold office in the Republic, but revolution itself was utterly abhorrent.

After the fall of the *Bloc des Gauches* the Radicals constituted the necessary foundation of any ministry and provided a good number of ministers, but as a party they were not in the driving seat. The key figures between 1906 and 1909 were the Prime Minister, Clemenceau, who was a member of the Radical party only in 1909, and Caillaux, the Finance Minister, who did not become a Radical until 1912. Caillaux had the reputation of a 'plutocratic demagogue', a man of private means and fine pedigree who was bent on disciplining the very wealthy in the interests of the public good. He had the support of the socialists and radical-socialists, but his policies were too extreme for moderate Radicals. His plan to nationalise the railway companies was pared down until it involved the nationalisation of only the bankrupt Western Railway, which Jaurès called 'a rotten egg'. His bill to establish progressive income tax, which was a fundamental reform of France's archaic direct tax system in order to tap the real sources of wealth, was also too much for many Radicals to stomach. The bill passed through the Chamber in March 1909, but Radicals felt secure in the hope that the Senate would oppose it. The bill was sent to a Senate commission chaired by Maurice Rouvier, a known adversary of income tax, where it was lost (**131**).

On the other hand Radicals were afraid of being seen too close to the Right. Increasingly they became dissatisfied with Clemenceau. He guaranteed order, but many thought that his tactics were unnecessarily brutal and even provocative. Clemenceau did not object to his image as the 'first cop in France', increasingly disassociated himself from his Finance Minister, and curried favour with the Democratic Alliance and the Republican Federation. In July 1909 a third of the Radicals voted against him and brought down his ministry. Clemenceau's successor, Briand, also sailed too close to the Right for the taste of Radicals. He was a former socialist now firmly in the moderate camp. In March 1910, with an eye to the elections of April and May, he and Viviani pushed through the pensions law which had been in the making for a decade. But when the railway workers went on strike in October Briand showed his true mettle by mobilising the strikers into the army. He too was accused by the Radicals of 'appeasing' the Right and was forced to resign and reconstitute his cabinet with more Radicals.

The Radicals prohibited consorting with the Right under the rules of republican legitimacy, but the rule of 'no enemies on the Left' could be difficult to follow. Moderate Radicals saw a solution in electoral reform: if single-member constituencies were replaced by proportional representation, the Radicals would no longer have to make electoral compromises with socialists and, their hands free, would be able to claim the middle ground between the socialists and the Right. However, successive party congresses rejected PR in favour of retaining the single-member constituency. There was a fear that PR would unduly favour the socialists, and even the Right, whereas under the existing system the socialists were required as often as not to stand down for the Radical candidate against the candidate of the Right according to the rules of republican discipline. There was a premium on keeping the formula which had produced Radical France.

Pressure was mounting from another direction to induce the Radicals to change the electoral system. The feminist movement was not only concerned with voting rights: Napoleon's Civil Code, which restricted the rights of women in questions of marriage and property, had long been an object of hatred. In 1904, when the French establishment was celebrating the centenary of the Code, a copy of it was burned in Paris by a group of feminists. In 1907 a law finally gave married French women control of their earnings. The suffrage movement tended to be the militant wing of feminism until 1908, when a French Union for Women's Suffrage was set up, dedicated to strive for the vote by 'moderate, bourgeois' means, to avoid the 'ridicule' to which the more violent British suffragettes exposed themselves. In 1906 a bill to give women the vote in local elections was introduced in the Chamber of Deputies, but there was little chance that it would make rapid progress. Radical rhetoric was all in favour of completing universal suffrage and democracy, and Ferdinand Buisson, author of the Radical programme and founder member of the League of Rights of Man, produced a report in favour of women's suffrage in 1909. But the decision on votes for women was subordinated to resolving the issue of PR. Clemenceau did not even try to seem open-minded. In a pamphlet published in 1907 he rehearsed old fears of the Catholic vote and the danger run by the Republic. 'If the right to vote were given to women tomorrow,' he stated, 'France would all of a sudden jump backwards into the Middle Ages' (**132**, p. 99).

The tension within the Radical party between radicalism and moderation was not resolved until the Radicals were rudely thrust from power. The Prime Minister, Caillaux, was accused of failing to protect France's interests against Germany at the time of the second Morocco crisis at the beginning of 1912 (which will be discussed in chapter 9) and obliged to resign. The victory was that of the moderates of the Democratic Alliance, with help from the Catholic Right. Poincaré became president of the council in January 1912, and he won over Albert de Mun and the Catholic Right by relaxing the lay laws, dissolving teachers' unions on the grounds of anti-patriotism, and gracing his civil marriage by a church wedding. He was elected president of the Republic with the help of the Right in January 1913. He appointed Briand, then Barthou, premier, and made a bid for nationalist support by strengthening the French army, increasing military service from two years to three.

Revenge came swiftly. Caillaux, cast from office, decided that the best way back was through a streamlined Radical party. He won the contest for the leadership at the Pau congress of October 1913, and introduced a programme which would slough off from the party those who were Radical in no more than name and make way for a tactical alliance with the SFIO in the elections of April 1914. The programme revolved round abrogation of the three-year military service law, defence of the lay school, and the establishment of progressive income tax. In December 1913 the new Radical-Socialist party and the SFIO overthrew Barthou, and Caillaux returned as Finance Minister in what was to be a caretaker government until the elections. Barthou and the moderates hired the *Figaro* to discredit Caillaux as a wheeler-dealer who had used ministerial office for private gain. When the press favourable to Caillaux rebutted all these charges, the *Figaro* prepared to expose his private life, notably his affair with his present second wife during his first marriage. Henriette Caillaux stopped the revelations by shooting the editor (**133**). The Radical-Socialists and

Analysis

SFIO triumphed in the elections of April 1914 and Caillaux and
Jaurès planned the formation of a joint ministry in the autumn.
However by then Caillaux's career, despite the acquittal of his
wife, was ruined; Jaurès was dead; and Europe was plunged into
war.

9 Nationalism

Defeat

The Third Republic was born out of the defeat of the Second Empire and was itself at once defeated by Prussia. It lived until 1914 under the shadow of defeat, but defeat had to be rationalised in order to make life bearable (**134**). 'The Frenchman,' said Trochu, the military governor of Paris during the Franco-Prussian war, 'has a special aptitude for explaining his defeats' (**134a**). Explanations were usually determined by interest or ideology. The republicans blamed ignorance: the French had been taught a lesson by the Prussian schoolmaster. They traced this ignorance to the 'obscurantism' of the Church schools and thus reinforced their argument for diminishing the Church's influence in education. 'We must put the gymnast and the soldier alongside the primary school teacher,' said Gambetta in 1871, to train 'a new generation, strong, intelligent, as enamoured of science as of the fatherland' (**134b**).

The Catholic Right interpreted defeat in a completely different way. They blamed the apostasy of the French nation, which in the last century had strayed from the ways of God. Its sins included liberalism, democracy, socialism, science and materialism, and the abandonment in 1870 of the Holy City of Rome which it had protected with its troops from revolution and nationalism since 1849. The scourges of Prussian soldiers (Protestant, materialist) and Communards (atheist, materialist) had been sent by God to chastise France. Only when the French repented and returned to the ways of God would God's grace be forthcoming. These sentiments were behind the subscription to build the basilica of Sacré-Cœur on the top of the Communard stronghold of Montmartre, pilgrimages to the shrines of Lourdes and Paray-le-Monial, and the revival of Catholic education under the Moral Order régime (**135**).

One explanation – apart from a purely military one – is more convincing than either of these. The propertied classes in France were not eager to fight. They feared that war, as in 1792, required mass mobilisation and that mass mobilisation might unleash revolutionary forces [**doc. 16**]. Paris was already seething when an armistice with Prussia was sought by what Marx ironically called 'the Government of National Defection' (**136**). While Gambetta wanted war to the death with Prussia, involving a *levée en masse*, Thiers and his allies wanted a truce with Prussia in order to bring Paris under control (**8**). The Paris Commune was a revolutionary and patriotic response to reactionaries and *capitulards*. In turn Thiers hurried to finalise peace terms so that French prisoners of war would be free to cross Prussian lines to suppress the Commune (**10**). There were few wars fought by France after the Revolution which were not civil wars as well.

Grandeur in a Republic?

It was a commonplace from the time of Montesquieu that monarchies were characterised by *grandeur* and republics by virtue. Thinkers like Ernest Renan, in the wake of the defeat of 1870, argued that *grandeur* was impossible in a republic. There was, however, a tradition of republican greatness which established France as a *Grande Nation*, more powerful than that of Louis XIV, before she became an Empire in 1804. Republican patriotism combined the ideas of civic virtue and the defence of the French *patrie*, the land of liberty. A fortnight after the proclamation of the Third Republic Victor Hugo wrote, 'The lion of 1792 is raising itself'. The war of 1870 was not without its heroes and heroism: the defence of Belfort was marked by the statue of a lion dedicated to the commander, Denfert-Rochereau, in Paris.

Republican patriotism and the aspiration to greatness was perpetuated after 1870 in the desire for *revanche*, or revenge, against Germany. However, there was some disagreement among the French as to the purpose of revenge. For the republicans it meant the recovery of Alsace and Lorraine, the eastern provinces which had been annexed by Germany. For the Catholic Right on the other hand it was to restore the Papal States, annexed by united Italy, to the Pope. This was intolerable to Bismarck, because the unity of the new German Reich was threatened by a Catholic periphery stretching from Alsace-Lorraine and Bavaria to the Polish provinces, and particularism aroused by a Catholic crusade in Italy might break it apart. Bismarck was happy to lend propaganda support to the republicans after the 16 May crisis, and the warning of the German ambassador in Paris, 'Ultramontanism means war'

(**137**, pp. 161–2) was echoed by Gambetta's 'Clericalism, there is the enemy' (**13**, p. 396). The republicans now projected themselves as the party of peace, against the Catholic Right, which would risk another war with Germany. It has been argued that the republicans were to some extent beholden to Bismarck for their victory in 1877 (**137**). Even if they were not, their policy meant that *revanche* had to be put on ice. The statue of Strasbourg in the Place de la Concorde draped in black, the schoolmaps of France with Alsace-Lorraine blotted out, Daudet's tear-jerking story, *The Last Lesson*, in which the French teacher, about to cede his class to a German teacher, consoles his pupils, were only so many symbols to satisfy French honour. Gradually references to the Rhine as a French river disappeared from textbooks (**138**), and battalions of school children who marched around with wooden rifles in preparation for *revanche* were disbanded.

The strategy of the republican oligarchy was to recover French honour by a route which did not involve antagonising Germany – the acquisition of colonies [**doc. 17a**]. Indeed Bismarck actually gave France a helping hand in establishing a protectorate in Tunisia in 1881, if mainly for his own reasons – to frighten Italy (whose interests in Tunisia were thus overridden) into an alliance with Germany and Austria-Hungary (**139**). The search for colonies was not all plain sailing. France was squeezed out of Egypt by the British in 1882, and recovered some dignity only by taking over a portion of the Congo, surrendered by King Makoko to the explorer de Brazza (**140**). Neither was the acquisition of colonies very popular, especially in the 1880s, when the critics of the Opportunists argued that it was wasteful (except for a minority of profiteers) and liable to involve France in colonial wars [**doc. 17b**] (**32**). When colonialism did become popular, in the 1890s, because it was seen as a projection of European Great Power rivalry, it was not particularly successful, as the Fashoda incident demonstrated.

The army

The army was both the fighting force of the Republic and a political entity. Despite the *coups d'état* of 1799 and 1851 France did not have a tradition of intervention of the military in politics, although the loyalty of the army to the Republic was sometimes open to question. The officer corps was not an aristocratic caste – 38 per cent of divisional generals were noble in 1876–8, 19 per cent in 1901, and the proportion was lower further down the hierarchy. But many officers had served previous regimes, including those imperial officers who had been captured at Metz and Sedan in 1870 and then reintegrated into the army. According to Gambetta's files in 1874–5, 88 per cent of divisional generals were hostile to the Republic (**142**). The problem did not diminish with retirements. Those of doubtful loyalty to the Republic were excluded by the republicans from politically sensitive posts in the administration and magistrature and had little choice of career apart from the army. Moreover, the military academy of Saint-Cyr recruited increasingly from Catholic colleges, which educated a social elite ill-disposed to the state *lycées*, forging the alliance, as the epithet had it, of 'the sabre and the holy-water sprinkler' (**142**).

The army had a role internally as well as externally, as a guarantor of social order. In some ways it was better at this than at winning battles. The shame of surrender to the Prussians was in part redeemed by the suppression of the Commune. The revolutionary force in Paris, the National Guard, was disbanded in 1871, and the army reform of 1872 deliberately avoided the model of the nation-in-arms, which Thiers described as 'putting a gun on the shoulder of every socialist' (**143**). Military service was made compulsory, but it was not universal or short-term. There were many exemptions and half the contingent did five years' service while the other half, which could not be accommodated, did six months. The aim of the republicans when they came to power was to integrate the army more with the nation, making it less like a standing army (**144**). Boulanger as War Minister planned the reduction of military service to three years and claimed, during the miners' strike at Décazeville, that each soldier was sharing his ration of soup with a miner. The *Bloc des Gauches* cut military service again in 1904 to two years. Nevertheless the inadequacy of the *gendarmerie* meant that the army was regularly used to control strikes and demonstrations. A bill to form a mobile corps of 2,000 *gendarmes* in April 1906 failed to pass the Chamber; the Left saw it as the instrument of *coups d'état*, while the Right feared it would become a tool of anticlericalism, to clear protesting Catholics from schools and churches. The pugnacious Clemenceau perhaps had no choice but to employ the army against the labour movement in 1906–8, but in no sense did he pull his punches (**145**).

Anti-militarism and a cult of the army co-existed in the generation before the war. The other ranks had always been brutally treated, but the military service law of 1889 constrained to service many sons of educated middle-class families who would previously have been exempt. The following years saw a rash of anti-military novels which criticised mindless discipline and the privileges of the officer corps (**146**). At the same time the military were scoring a number of victories in Indo-China and Africa, such as the conquest of Madagascar in 1896, which fired the popular imagination. The popular press was full of stories and images (some less than authentic) of the atrocities of races and regimes in hotter climates and of the benefits of Western civilisation brought by the soldier and the missionary (**147**). The Dreyfus Affair was a confrontation of these two perspectives. For some, military justice beyond the purview of the civil courts was the epitome of military privilege and tyranny over individual rights which had been sanctified by the French Revolution. For others, military justice could not be questioned without weakening the army and France itself. These found it difficult to believe that in the same army that took part in manoeuvres and marches with bridles jangling and flags fluttering there were officers who were forging documents in back rooms. The view that a 'syndicate' of Jews and intellectuals were out to rubbish it was easily believed. Now that the monarchy had been abolished, the army – albeit the army of the Republic – was seen to represent the present embodiment of a glorious past which should be set apart and idolised.

Nationalist movements

The nationalist movements which emerged at the time of the Dreyfus Affair attacked the supine attitude of the government toward Great Britain. But they were not in favour of war. They were opposed to the republican oligarchy which had monopolised power for twenty years and used the rhetoric of the Republic in danger to keep office within their own magic circle. Every attempt to open the 'closed' Republic, whether by threat or blandishment, had failed. Boulangism and the Panama scandal had not swept them away. Those moderates who had bowed to the republican regime had found some sympathy from Méline, but after the elections of 1898 Méline was out of power and the door firmly closed on them by the radicals. The new strategy of the opposition was to attack the republican political class as anti-French or non-French. It was accused of being a minority which did not truly reflect French opinion but which had perfected a machinery for taking and retaining power. It was accused also of peddling foreign

Analysis

ideologies and betraying France's interests to the foreigner. The
opposition sought to marginalise the ruling elite and claim for itself
a legitimacy based on the representation of French interests and
Frenchness.

The identification of the republican oligarchy with the Jews went
back to Drumont's *La France juive*. In 1898 and 1899 the smear of
Protestantism and Freemasonry was also liberally applied. The
Protestants were portrayed as a party which had organised the
conquest of power under the Republic, as a community which had
been emancipated at the Revolution and turned to persecute the
Catholic Church, and as a fifth column, if not a foreign, Germanic,
race, which had served the interests of Prussia and Great Britain
since the sixteenth century (**148**). The Freemasons were similarly
criticised as machine men, the wire-pullers behind the Radical
party, as anticlerical, anti-military and (since they belonged to an
international confraternity) as indifferent patriots.

If the republican oligarchy did not fit into any of these categories, then they were associated with the intellectuals and
academics who had mounted the Dreyfus Affair. This was the basic
theme of the writings of Maurice Barrès. Barrès argued that these
'aristocrats of thought' regarded the masses as stupid and traditional. They wanted to uproot the masses from their past and their
backgrounds in order to bring them into the bright light of republican morality and patriotism. The unity of France would be forged
in the classroom; France was nothing but 'a set of ideas'.
Barrès's view was that intellectuals should grasp the contradiction
of trying to convert stupid people to their republican philosophy.
In any case, though the masses might be stupid in their terms,
there were untold treasures in 'the national unconscious, the sure
instinct of the masses'. That unconscious was determined by forces
which preceded and enfolded the individual, the weight of heredity
and environment. To try to uproot people from these influences
was to defy reality. Instead those who were looking to restore the
'moral unity' of France should accept these determining forces.
Nationalism for Barrès thus became the cult of the forces which
had made the French: ancestors and soil. National feeling was
created among the crowds who attended the funeral of Victor
Hugo in 1885, in those who descended the valley of the Moselle,
or in those who visited the war cemeteries of 1870, where French
blood and soil were mingled (**149**).

Some historians have argued that nationalism switched at the
turn of the century from being a doctrine on the Left to being a

doctrine on the Right (**150**). In fact, the main development was that a patriotism which identified France with the Republic was challenged by a nationalism which disconnected France and the Republic. This nationalism claimed that France's true interests were not represented by the politicians who currently held power in the Republic. That did not mean that they were opposed to the Republic as a regime, but it made possible a rapprochement under the nationalist banner of those who had different views about the regime. For instance, both strict republicans and Bonapartists could agitate in Déroulède's *Ligue des Patriotes*. The *Ligue de la Patrie Française* by and large subscribed to the ideas of Barrès: nationalist without being racist, given the Flemish, Breton and Basque elements in the French nation; and not loyal to a particular dynasty, for the French had lived under monarchies, empires and republics, and were still French. There was one exception to this rule. The *Action Française*, which was born under the wing of the *Ligue de la Patrie Française*, originally grouped Bonapartists and radicals who had refused to follow Clemenceau into the Dreyfusard camp, and demanded a strong authoritarian (instead of a parliamentary) Republic. But in 1900 it came under the influence of Charles Maurras, an admirer of Renan, who saw the salvation of France only in the restoration of the monarchy. His argument was not sentimental but, in his view, ruthlessly logical. All the Great European Powers, according to Maurras, were monarchies; France was not great and she was a republic; therefore France could recover greatness only if she restored the monarchy [**doc. 18**].

Towards the *Union Sacrée*

In 1904 the Entente Cordiale settled the rivalry between France and Great Britain in Africa – France recognised Britain's supremacy in Egypt, while Britain recognised France's interest in Morocco. Now France faced the challenge of German power and pretensions, and her greatness was put squarely to the test. In 1905 Germany took advantage of the defeat of France's ally, Russia, at the hands of the Japanese and the ensuing revolution in Russia to provoke France into war over her Moroccan ambitions. France stood firm, with the support of Great Britain, but from this moment the possibility of war with the old enemy, Germany, was a fact of French life.

The crisis gave a boost to nationalist groups (**151**). The *Action Française* launched a daily paper of the same name in 1908, which was hawked about by street runners, the *Camelots du Roy*, who doubled as hit squads for such occasions as the transfer of the ashes of the reviled Zola to the Panthéon. But popular anti-militarism was also stimulated. An International Anti-militarist Association was set up at Amsterdam in 1904. It had links with the CGT and socialists like Gustave Hervé who argued that the workers had no country but their class and should respond to any mobilisation order by a general strike. The authorities clamped down heavily on such people. Hervé's career, first as a barrister, then as a schoolmaster, was ruined. Anti-militarists who undertook propaganda among conscripts were sent for trial in December 1905. However anti-militarism was not the same as anti-patriotism, as proclaimed by Hervé. Hervéism was rejected in 1906 by the CGT at its Amiens congress and by the SFIO meeting at Limoges. Jaurès himself was an anti-militarist, in that he opposed long-service armies which could be used to stage *coups d'état*, to put down strikes and to start colonial wars; but – not least to maintain links with the Radicals – he tried to reconcile socialism and patriotism. France, he said, was the *patrie* – the land of liberty – and must be defended against invasion not for chauvinistic French interests but for the benefit of Humanity. The workers had been at the forefront of national defence in 1792–3 and 1870–1, while aristocrats and bourgeois treated with the enemy. And the more socialists achieved reforms in France, the more France would become the patrimony of the working class. Anti-militarism and patriotism could be reconciled if France organised a citizen army which would defend the *patrie* but would not let itself be used for strike-breaking, *coups* or wars of aggression. This was the burden of Jaurès's book, *L'Armée nouvelle*, in 1910.

The Left was anti-militarist but with few exceptions patriotic in the Jacobin sense [**doc. 19**]. Nationalism permitted the Right to criticise the republicans in power and to claim that it rather than they represented true French interests. Republicans were still divided from the Right by anticlericalism, but the Separation of Church and State ended the political threat posed by the Church and opened the way for Catholicism to become an integral part of French nationalism. Péguy was able to reconcile patriotism with Catholicism through the cult of Joan of Arc, who was beatified (the second step to canonisation) in 1909 (**152**). Barrès was led by his cult of blood and soil to realise that the French past was Catholic, symbolised by its cathedrals, and that the Catholicism of Alsace-Lorraine (ignoring its Lutheran and Jewish populations) had for forty years been the most important factor preventing its full integration into the German Reich. Interest in the lost provinces revived, stimulated by plays and writings including Barrès's cycle of novels, *Les Bastions de l'Est*, and Hansi's best-selling illustrated history of Alsace, in which the Germans all have red noses. But the interest in Alsace-Lorraine was above all in France. The foundation of a Catholic university at Strasbourg in 1902, insulation against Combist persecution, and a constitution in 1911 which enlarged both provincial and federal representation effectively reconciled the inhabitants of Alsace-Lorraine to the Reich (**153**).

The second Morocco crisis of 1911–12 seemed to be a gift to the Right. Caillaux preserved the peace and Morocco for the French by ceding some of the French Congo but was then chased from office on the grounds that he had failed to protect French interests. Nationalist agitation reached a peak both in France and Germany (**154**). Maurras published a pamphlet called *Kiel and Tangiers*, in which he argued that the monarchy had to be restored if France were to stand up to Germany. Albert de Mun, who had been instrumental in the fall of Caillaux, was also instrumental in the rise of Poincaré to the presidency of the Republic (**155**), and he exacted notable concessions for Catholics along the way. This did not mean that the Right was obtaining power through the back door. Poincaré strengthened the presidency by the force of his character and because foreign relations, which were the president's affair, had become all-important. But Maurras's argument was correspondingly weakened. Poincaré as President of the Republic, observed Péguy, was a republican monarch; with him the French had all the advantages of monarchy and none of the risks. Moreover Poincaré's ministers, though moderate, had impeccable republican credentials. Not even when war broke out in 1914 was a non-republican of any shade given office (although one or two names were considered).

The overthrow of Barthou in December 1913 and the defeat of his party in April 1914 was a blow to Poincaré's system. The Radicals and SFIO triumphed with the commitment to abrogate the three-year military service law and put progressive income tax on the statute book. The ex-socialist Viviani became Prime Minister. But given the international crisis, the ministry agreed to retain the three-year law if the Senate agreed to progressive income tax. Poincaré went to St Petersburg to ensure the solidarity of Russia. Popular opinion (when the end of Madame Caillaux's trial allowed it to focus on events outside France), was massively hostile to Austrian aggression, supported by Germany, in the Balkans. If the CGT and SFIO had wanted to resist war by a general strike, they would have been swept away. Instead, they rallied to the defence of the Republic (**156, 157, 158**). Guesde, the revolutionary, accepted office. In the face of the enemy all classes and all parties rallied in what was dubbed the *Union Sacrée* (**159**). The conflicts of the Third Republic were suspended, not resolved, but for the moment France was united, and in the course of the next four years, republic would avenge itself against monarchy on the battlefield.

Part Three: Conclusion

10 The Third Republic Assessed

The Third Republic has never had a very good press. It is often seen as one of those liberal, democratic regimes like Weimar Germany which, although tolerant and well-meaning, was unable to withstand the challenge of less savoury politics and more aggressive neighbours. The Republic, it is true, crumbled before the tanks and air-power of Nazi Germany in 1940, and the life of the Republic after the Great War was no doubt less happy than it had been before 1914. However this should not blind us to the clear evidence that before 1914 the Third Republic was a viable government and a stable society.

Three criticisms are regularly made of the Third Republic. First that under it France was a backward country economically, at least by western European standards. Second that it was politically unstable, and riven by outdated ideological quarrels. And third that the Republic was by nature unpatriotic, and a weakling in the society of nations.

The first criticism is that France was economically backward. France's population was increasing very slowly, and in 1911 was 39 million to Germany's 65 million. France was described as a peasant society, one of small, inefficient farms and sleepy villages. It was said that industrial workers were recruited from the countryside and dreamed of returning there to raise hens and rabbits. Industry counted for little in the gross national product, and was characterised by artisans making luxury articles and family firms in which the business existed to maintain the family rather than the other way round. It was a country without a proletariat, and France was a society of *rentiers*, who invested their savings not in industry but in government stock and above all in land. The ambition of the *bourgeois* was to retire to the countryside and relax on the income from his vineyard.

This view is partly a nostalgic self-image of the French, that of Marcel Pagnol and Gabriel Chevallier's *Clochemerle* (1934), and partly the view of American scholars like Laurence Wylie who discovered France after the Second World War (**160**), and were charmed by a society so different from their own. There is a danger that remembrance of things past will become caricature, and it is. as well to recall some of the more dynamic features of French economic life. Agriculture was clearly in the doldrums, with a growth-rate of 0.5 per cent per annum between 1880 and 1913. But after the depression of the 1880s, there was a spurt of 1 per cent per annum between 1895 and 1913, which was as high as in the prosperous middle decades of the century, and farm incomes rose markedly after 1895, largely in response to rising demand from the towns. In industry, similarly, between the 1860s and the end of the century there was a slackening of growth, which averaged about 1.5 per cent per annum. But after 1895, and particularly between 1906 and 1929, there was an economic *Belle Epoque* during which industrial growth amounted to 5 per cent per annum. In some sectors, such as coal and textiles, growth was unspectacular, but progress was fast in the newest sectors – iron and steel, engineering, electricity, electrochemicals and electrometallurgy. The old crafts of the artisans became high-tech enterprises, as when carriage-making mutated into the automobile industry. In 1913 France was making 45,000 vehicles a year. New sources of power were being developed to supply these new industries, particularly hydroelectric power in the Alpine region around Grenoble. The engineers trained by France's elite technical schools moved aggressively into the private sector after 1890, headed the new industries and undertook vast projects such as the electrification of the transport and lighting system of Paris. And though industry continued to be 80 per cent self-financing, banks were becoming much more interested in industrial investment, and between 1895 and 1906 industry's share of the stock issue on the Paris Stock Exchange rose from half to two-thirds (**161**).

The second main accusation brought against the Republic is that it was politically unstable. In particular it is demonstrated that ministries came and went in the Italian style, and that France lacked strong leadership. The truth is that France had made a deliberate choice against both monarchy and Empire, which at various times since the Revolution had shown contempt for constitutional, parliamentary forms of government. The Third Republic was a parliamentary Republic and designed as such. The president was elected by parliament and was not allowed to dissolve the Chamber of Deputies without the agreement of the Senate precisely so that the *coup d'état* of 1851 should not happen again. There was continuity in the predominance of a certain political class which threw up men of undoubted quality: Jules Ferry, René Waldeck-Rousseau, and Théophile Delcassé, to name but a few. When a more presidential style was appropriate, as on the eve of the First World War, parliament found a man who clearly had the weight and authority to be an assertive president, Raymond Poincaré. Georges Clemenceau, remembered by history as the Tiger, was in fact one of the most destructive politicians of the Third Republic, known in the 1880s as the 'toppler of ministries'. It says much that he was denied the highest office, but that Poincaré, who disliked and mistrusted Clemenceau, nevertheless appreciated his undoubted quality and asked him to form a government to win the war in 1917.

Criticism of the parliamentary nature of the Republic tends to focus either on the rule of party or on the alleged corruption of the regime. But it should be remembered that this criticism was not always objective, and was often motivated by particular interest. One scathing critic of the rule of party, for example, was General de Gaulle, who resigned from the provisional government of the Fourth Republic in 1946 because the parties were about to make another parliamentary constitution. But that system worked so well that De Gaulle was not called back from the political wilderness until the Algerian problem finished off the Fourth Republic twelve years later. Even then, in framing the constitution of the Fifth Republic in 1958, he was careful not to reject indirect elections to the presidency which had been enshrined since 1875, for fear that memories of 1848 and 1851 would be revived. When he did institute direct presidential elections in 1962, they were indeed revived. There was always a broad body of support for the parliamentary republic, and not only from politicians.

Attacks on the corruption of the Third Republic – and in particular on the manipulation of politicians by finance and the press – were very common at the time. Maupassant, for instance, exposed it cleverly in his novel *Bel Ami* (1885). Yet many of these criticisms came from members of the Right like Maurice Barrès, who had been excluded from power by the republican political class. Their bitterness was in part the sour grapes of those who had been cast out of the charmed circles of political patronage since the events of 1877.

The absence of *alternance* in power between Left and Right was a fundamental fact of political life in the Third Republic and an option that was deliberately excluded by the republicans (**17**). This is a much more promising target for attack, and it is worth inves-

Conclusion

tigating whether anything can be said in defence of the Republic's exclusivism.

The first justification is that the battle was fought in the realm of ideology, not of force. During the First Republic, the republicans had resorted to force in 1795 and 1797 when the royalists threatened to win parliamentary elections. Under the constitution of 1875 the royalists never came near to winning a parliamentary majority. The republicans accused them of plotting counter-revolution; but this was by and large a rhetorical device, which served the cause of raising the spectre of tithes and feudal dues before the eyes of the peasantry and thus induced them to support the Republic. Positive benefits accrued also, such as universal suffrage, free elementary education, and railway branch lines. During the election campaign of 1885 Jules Ferry declared that the republicans had won the democratic support of the countryside, and reminded his audience that the peasants owed their untroubled property rights to the Revolution.

The ideology of Jacobinism, which placed the regime, the Catholic Church and the army at the centre of political debate and excluded other issues – especially social issues – from consideration, has been seen as the sterile reworking of arguments which rightfully belonged to the French Revolution. There is some truth in this. The claims of the working class and women were repeatedly subordinated to the pursuit of traditional quarrels. Just when it seemed that new issues were forcing their way to the front, in the 1890s, for example, the Dreyfus Affair drove the politicians back to familiar battle lines.

However, it would be untrue to say that the Third Republic enacted no social programme. Women's rights in matters of education, property and marriage were extended, even if the vote eluded them before 1945. Trade union rights, factory acts, accident insurance and pensions were established for the working classes, paid for by progressive taxes on inheritance and income. Some price had to be paid for the entry of radicals and socialists into the Jacobin coalition. Sometimes that price was too high, and it seemed as if the republicans would relax the rules of republican legitimacy and enter a partnership with the moderate Right. There were signs of this under Rouvier in 1887, and under Méline in 1896–8. Poincaré was elected president with support from the Right. Many politicians who bore the label of the Left were effectively on the Right in terms of the policies they pursued. Clemenceau was the great strike-breaker of 1906–8, Caillaux as leader of the Senate was the arch-enemy of the Popular Front in the 1930s, Millerand became a conservative president of the Republic after the war, and the working-class constituents of Briand used to read his early anarchist speeches at uproarious drinking parties. But politicians of the traditional Right, however liberal they became, never gained office before 1914, and the return of the Right had to await what Maurras called the 'divine surprise' of 1940.

Before the First World War the republican political class was able to play on its revolutionary heritage to keep the labour movement bound tightly in alliance, and when that failed, it could bend its own rules to make some sort of working compromise with the Right. Both of these options became more difficult in the wake of the Bolshevik Revolution of 1917. On the one hand the Communist Party broke with the Socialist Party and ballooned on the extreme left. (The socialists, instead of becoming more 'social democratic' in fact moved further to the left in pursuit of the same voters as the Communists: the socialists refused to enter a government with the Radicals until 1936.) On the other hand Bolshevism created its own enemy at the other end of the political spectrum – Fascism. Even if French Fascism was not on the same scale and of the same nature as Fascism in Italy or Germany, it transformed the nature of the Right in France and ruled out bridge-building on the model of the *Ralliement*.

The third criticism of the Third Republic is that it was unpatriotic and not quite a Great Power. At various times before 1914, Catholics were accused of being more loyal to the Papacy than to France and of being happy to see the godless Republic roundly chastised; intellectuals were accused of undermining the army and thus the ability of France to defend itself; primary school teachers were accused of inculcating anti-patriotic sentiments in the classroom; and workers were accused of planning a general strike and revolution in the event of war being declared. However, these accusations tended to derive from groups which sought to appropriate a monopoly of nationalism and to denounce their opponents as defeatists. There was a patriotism of the Left and one of the Right. The Dreyfusard intellectuals wanted a France which would defend the Rights of Man, and not subordinate them to *raison d'état*. Anti-militarism and even anti-imperialism did not necessarily entail anti-patriotism. The workers were ready to leap to the defence of France against the 'Boches'. On the Left the defence of France meant the defence of the Republic. The Right was critical of the Republic and keen to demonstrate that France was more than the Republic. After the Separation of Church and State, it was easier to argue that Catholicism was a potent ingredient of French national consciousness. In August 1914, unlike in May–June 1940, France held together. The International was washed away by the tide of popular patriotism, anticlerical legislation was suspended, and chaplains accompanied the infantrymen to the front. The *Union Sacrée* was established.

Neither did France demonstrate any great weakness in 1914. The first onslaught of the German military was checked on the Marne in September and the Schlieffen Plan which for a generation had projected a war by timetable by which Germany could defeat France *and* Russia was consigned to the rubbish-tip of history. The fortress of Verdun was held in 1916. The German offensive of 1918 was again stopped on the Marne. Between 1914 and 1918 France mobilised 8.4 million men, thousands of whom were carried to the front by 'the taxis of the Marne'. It was a war fought by the French people. 1.35 million died and 3.5 million were wounded; nearly 60 per cent of those mobilised were killed or wounded (**162**). There is scarcely a village in France without its war memorial, more often than not one showing a *poilu* (as the infantryman was called) sinking into the flag. By comparison Great Britain and the United States lost 950,000 and 100,000 men respectively. In 1919, in the Hall of Mirrors of the Chateau of Versailles, France redeemed the humiliating defeat of 1870 and the proclamation of the German Empire in that same hall in 1871, and imposed a resounding peace – including the recovery of Alsace-Lorraine – on the successor of the German Empire, the Weimar Republic.

Part Four: Documents

Note: all texts except 1(b) have been translated by the author.

document 1

Two views of popular sovereignty

Republicans stood for popular sovereignty but had to reckon with the fact that universal suffrage was upheld by the Second Empire. The main dispute with the Empire and among liberals and republicans was how that popular sovereignty should be exercised. In document (a), Gambetta tells his electors of Belleville, in the Paris suburbs, of the need to organise a firm parliamentary Left to establish responsible but still parliamentary government. In document (b), on the eve of the Commune, the central committee of delegates from vigilance committees in each of the twenty arrondissements of Paris shows itself suspicious of all parliamentary representation.

(a) We must organise a Left, composed exclusively of citizens who have rallied to the same principles.

The idea is not to purge but to make uniform; we must decompose the current Left into two parts and between them draw a line of demarcation which from now on will prevent confusion, without ruling out good-neighbourly relations and occasional co-operation.

The first fraction includes the supporters of constitutional monarchy. All those who believe that universal suffrage may be reconciled with *necessary liberties* must put themselves under the orders of M. Thiers and his friends, and resolutely pursue the restoration of pure parliamentarism. The other fraction will now be made up uniquely of those who think that the people is the only true and only legitimate sovereign, but that it requires the reality of power; those who, with Favre, Simon, Bancel, Pelletan, and the others think and say that the people will be satisfied only when they have demoted their masters to the rank of fully obedient and responsible subalterns . . .

In short, they believe that the country will have neither order, security or liberty until a fully emancipated universal suffrage has founded democratic institutions which of themselves will ensure liberty, equality and fraternity.

Letter of Gambetta to the electors of the first constituency of the Seine, 28 July 1869, in *Discours et Plaidoyers politiques*, vol. i, Paris, 1881, pp. 432–3.

(b) Every member of a vigilance committee declares his adherence to the Revolutionary-Socialist Party. Consequently he demands and seeks to obtain by all means possible the elimination of the privileges of the bourgeoisie, its elimination as a governing caste, and the assumption of political power by the workers. In a word: social equality. No more employers, no more proletariat, no more classes. He recognises labour as the sole foundation of the social order and believes that the full product of labour should belong to the worker.

In the area of politics he places the existence of the Republic above the question of majority rule. Consequently he does not recognise the right of any majority to deny the principle of popular sovereignty, whether by plebiscite or indirectly, or by any assembly that would represent such a majority. He will therefore oppose, by force if necessary, the convocation of any constituent or alleged National Assembly that would occur before the foundations of the present social order have been altered decisively through political and social revolutionary change.

Until this definitive revolution shall have occurred, he recognises as the government of the city only the revolutionary Commune emanating from the delegation of the revolutionary-socialist groups of this same city.

Declaration of principles of the Delegation of the Twenty *Arrondissements*, 19 February 1871, in Eugene Schulkind, *The Paris Commune of 1871*, 1972, pp. 90–1.

document 2

Two views of royalist restoration

The main obstacle in the way of a royalist restoration was the gulf which separated the Pretender in exile from the royalist politicians in France. Document (a) is the famous manifesto of the Comte de Chambord on 5 July 1871; document (b) is a programme drawn up by the royalist majority of the

National Assembly, hammered together in difficult negotiations between the royalist factions, but rejected by Chambord.

(a) No, just because the ignorant and credulous have spoken of privileges, absolutism, intolerance and, what else? Of tithes and feudal dues, spectres which the most audacious bad faith is trying to raise before your eyes, I will not let the standard of Henri IV, of Francis I and of Joan of Arc be snatched from my grasp. With that flag national unity was achieved. I received it like a sacred trust from the old king, my forefather [Charles X], dying in exile. For me it has always been inseparable from the memory of my absent country; it has floated over my cradle, and I wish it to shade my tomb. I will bring you order and liberty in the glorious folds of this unsullied standard. People of France! Henri V cannot abandon the white flag of Henri IV.

Manifesto of the Comte de Chambord, 5 July 1871, cited in Comte de Falloux, *Mémoires d'un Royaliste*, vol. II, Paris, 1888, pp. 481–2.

(b) We consider monarchy to be the natural government of the country, and by monarchy we understand traditional hereditary monarchy. Monarchy has made France, and for centuries given her stability and greatness. In 1789 it anticipated reforms spontaneously, and in 1814 it both founded liberty and safeguarded territorial integrity. A hereditary, representative, constitutional monarchy assures the country the right to participate in the running of its own affairs, and under the guarantee of ministerial responsibility assures all the necessary liberties – political, civil, religious, equality before the law, free access to all professions, to all honours and to all social advantages, and the peaceful and continuous improvement of the condition of the working classes.

Programme of the Right, cited in Duc d'Audiffret-Pasquier, *La Maison de France et l'Assemblée Nationale. Souvenirs, 1871–1873*, Paris, 1938, pp. 54–5.

document 3

A conservative Republic?

In this address to the National Assembly the consummate politician Thiers tries to establish the Republic as a regime beyond questioning by the Right, but at the same time warns that anarchy and radical party politics will serve only to improve the chances of Bonapartism. His plea is for a sober parliamentary Republic which will represent the Nation.

The Republic exists, it is the legal government of the country; to want anything else would be a new revolution and the most fearful of all. Let us not waste time declaring it, but use the time to impress upon it desirable and necessary characteristics. A commission appointed by you a few months ago gave it the title of conservative Republic. Let us seize that title and strive to deserve it. (*'Hear, hear!'*)

Every government must be conservative and no society can live under a government which is not. (*General agreement.*) The Republic will be conservative, or it will not exist. (*Exclamations.*)

A VOICE ON THE CENTRE LEFT: Hear, hear! We'll buy that!

THE PRESIDENT OF THE REPUBLIC: France does not want to live in continual crisis. She wishes to live at peace, to work to feed herself and to meet the huge obligations [German reparations] placed upon her. And if she is not given the peace she so badly needs, the government which fails to give her peace, whatever it is, will not long be tolerated! (*'That's right!' 'Hear, hear!' on a large number of benches on the left and centre left.*) Let us have no illusions. It may be thought that it is possible to found a republic which is that of a party, based on the power of the many, thanks to universal suffrage. Such a republic would not last a day.

Even the many need rest, security and work. (*'That's right!' 'Hear, hear!'*) . . . Having made others afraid, they become afraid of themselves, throw themselves into the arms of an opportunist dictator and pay for a few days of disastrous licence with twenty years of slavery. (*'That's right, that's right!' Prolonged applause on many benches.*)

Yes, let us break the chain which links these two evil opposites, and make peace instead of disorder. Let us make the necessary sacrifices for general security, even sacrifices which may seem excessive, and above all let us not so much as glimpse the rage of party.

The Revolution of 1789 was made so that there would be no more classes, so that in the nation there would be only the nation itself, living entirely under the same law, bearing the same burdens, enjoying the same advantages, in which all, in a word, were rewarded or punished according to their deeds. (*'Hear, hear!' and applause on the left.*)

For myself, I understand and accept the Republic only as it

should be, as a government of the nation which, having for a long time and in good faith left the direction of its destinies to a hereditary power, which failed as a result of mistakes which we cannot assess today, decides to run its own affairs itself, through deputies freely and wisely elected, not according to party, or class, or origin, taking them neither from the top or the bottom, neither from the left nor the right, but in the light of public esteem, where character, qualities, defects cannot be mistaken, and choosing them with a freedom that can be enjoyed only in the midst of order, calm and security. (*Bravos and approval – acclamations – on the left.*)

Adolphe Thiers, Speech to National Assembly, 13 November 1872, *Journal Officiel de la République Française*, 14 November 1872, pp. 6981–2.

document 4
The establishment of republican legitimacy

In this speech on 16 June 1877, a month after the coup of 16 May and the day on which the Chamber of Deputies was dissolved by the President of the Republic with the approval of the Senate, Gambetta firmly denounces the Right as supporters of the old regime. It is a statement of republican legitimacy, in which those who claim the heritage of the French Revolution disqualify from office in the Republic those whom they argue cannot.

M. GAMBETTA – I am asking you whether the constitution has closed the era of revolutions, yes or no. Messieurs, I am fully aware – and this is precisely the grievance I am expressing about the ministers – I know only too well that those devoted servants of the policy of 16 May are the sworn enemies of the constitution. It is just that some dare not say it while others say and proclaim it daily.(*Applause on the left.*)
   . . . We are confronted by men who are not rooted in the constitution. These are not men who defend the constitution with their own particular style, though still in harmony with the spirit of the constitution. No! No! If that were the case, if there were a Whig party and a Tory party in the Republic, we could debate and engage in parliamentary politics. We could believe that the President has nothing but constitutional sentiments. But everyone knows that this is not the case. Everyone knows that it would be impossible for you [on the Right] to say with sincerity that there

is a single one among you who does not have a political ideal different from that which governs us today. (*Loud approval on the left.*)

Oh, Messieurs, make no mistake . . . it does not befit you, given your origins, to speak of the principles of 1789 (*Ironic outbursts on the left*) and to say that you favour equality. It would be something to hear you say here that you favour ducal supremacy and the oligarchy of a few nobles. (*'Hear, hear!' on the left.*)

Ah! You say that you endorse the French Revolution! In that case I will declare before the country that you can be called only one thing: you are called the counter-revolution. (*'Hear, hear!' on the left and centre.*) You can bear nothing but that name because today, as in 1830 . . . we are confronted by nobles who will not accept democracy, and by a congregation [the Jesuit order] which wants to enslave France. (*Bravos and applause on the left.*)

Léon Gambetta, Speech to the Chamber of Deputies, 16 June 1877, in *Discours et Plaidoyers politiques de Gambetta*, vol. vii, Paris, 1882, pp. 125–6, 140.

Two views of parliamentary life

document 5

The parliamentary system of the Third Republic came in for a good deal of criticism. One of its most scathing critics was Maurice Barrès, a Boulangist in his youth, who later wrote a series of novels against the regime: Les Déracinés, L'Appel au Soldat, *and* Leurs Figures. *In document (a), an extract from the second novel, he puts the words of criticism into the mouth of the radical, later Boulangist, politician Naquet. But the parliamentary system must have been in the interests of many people, as Robert de Jouvenel explains in document (b), from* La République des Camarades, *originally published in 1914.*

(a) The evil lies in parliamentary institutions. A regime which places ministers in the Chamber sterilises them; we are for ever discussing not what is on the order paper but the fall or survival of the cabinet. The question of confidence is posed at every step, which perverts all debates and inhibits the free vote. How can deputies be free when ministers force them to opt between a vote for them and a ministerial crisis? Which deputy would refuse to support a minister from whom he was requesting the gift of tax collectorships or tobacconists' licences? And how can he avoid making these requests when electors know the decisive influence of a deputy on the choice of ministers and insist that he gets to work for them on pain of non-re-election? Private interests take precedence over the public interest and the administration falls apart. The way to end this deplorable state of affairs would be to separate administration from legislation, to confine parliament to making laws and let ministers enforce them. That, sirs, is what we are going to do with General Boulanger.

Maurice Barrès, *L'Appel au Soldat*, Livre de Poche, p. 122.

(b) When you become a deputy, you can have only one pressing preoccupation: to remain one.

The difficulty varies between constituency and constituency. In some regions, it is enough to hold the office in order to keep it.

'That deputy is already well greased,' say electors in some distant provinces, whereas of a new one they say, 'he will have to be greased.'

I'm not sure whether that isn't the last word of wisdom, so far as universal suffrage is concerned.

Elsewhere, on the other hand, they like new faces. There it is most difficult to keep one's seat.

To keep your seat, there is only one essential rule: think about it all the time. The deputy who is always thinking about it must divide his time between three principal tasks: running errands, making promises, and writing.

If his errands bear no fruit, if his promises are always empty and if his letters never achieve anything definitive, that is only of minor importance. The elector who requests a service does not always insist on the deputy delivering. He wants 1. to demonstrate his importance; and 2. to receive letters.

A good deputy, who receives a letter from an elector, must straightaway write three:

One to the competent administration, to pass on the request of the interested party.

One to the interested party, to notify him that his request is being dealt with.

A second to the same, to advise him of the decision of the competent administration.

Deputies who receive forty letters a day from electors are not exceptional.

Parliament does not reign, does not govern, it writes. The regime which presides over our destinies is neither the Republic, nor the Empire, nor Royalty, nor autocracy, nor democracy – it is Correspondence.

Robert de Jouvenel, *La République des Camarades*, Bernard Grasset, Paris, 1934, pp. 22–4.

document 6
Anticlericalism: rhetoric and realism

These two documents illustrate different faces of anticlericalism. Document (a) is a speech by Gambetta on campaign in the south of France, not long after the 16 May crisis, which is clearly appreciated by his left-wing, robustly anticlerical audience. Document (b), from a speech delivered in parliament ten years later by the architect of the education reforms, Jules Ferry, is an attempt to stop anticlericalism short of the hurdle of disestablishment. He is attacked by the Left but can do nothing to gain the confidence of the Right.

(a) I am going to tackle a question which attracts passion and vehemence: the clerical question, the question of relations between Church and State. It is indeed a huge question, because it holds all other questions in suspense, because . . . within it lies the question of hostility to modern thought and the conflict which we have to resolve.

What has not been said on this issue? The inviolable domain of our consciences has been invaded and attempts have been made to interpret our policies in the dim light of our philosophy. I no more accept this position than I would accept that I can grasp the intimate sentiments of the religious conscience of a political adversary in order to attack his political standpoint. Even so I have the right to denounce the peril that is threatening French society, as it is constituted and as it wishes to be, from the growth of a spirit that is not merely clerical, but Vaticanesque, monastic, congregationist and syllabist [a reference to the Papal Syllabus of Errors of 1864]. It is a spirit that does not fear to subject the human mind to the crudest fabrications, disguised by the most subtle and profound arguments, which are those of ignorance trying to exploit slavishness in order to anchor itself. (*Long bursts of applause. Bravos and repeated shouts of: 'Long live Gambetta'.*)

. . . I do not simply want to take things from the point of view of party, which I do not recognise as valid for anyone, but from the governmental, public, and national point of view. In the light of ceaseless encroachment and usurpation by the clerical mind which is served by 40,000 regulars on top of the secular clergy, I have the right to say as I expose those masters of deceit who talk of the social peril: *there* is the social peril! (*Bursts of applause. Signs of unanimous agreement.*)

Léon Gambetta, speech at Romans, 18 September 1878, in *Discours et Plaidoyers politiques de Gambetta*, vol. viii, Paris, 1883, pp. 242–3.

(b) M. JULES FERRY – Messieurs, we remain profoundly attached to the lay school; and yet as I have had occasion to say in various circumstances and as I do not hesitate to say in this Assembly, we are most anxious to see religious peace reign in this country. (*Loud exclamations on the left. Applause in the centre.*)

M. LE COMTE DE MUN – Mr Speaker, I have restrained myself for three hours, I have not interrupted, but I surely have the right to say to the speaker that he is the last person here who can talk about religious peace. (*'Hear, hear!' on the right.*)

M. JULES FERRY – Messieurs, there are three questions in this country which concern religious peace: the question of religious associations, the question of the state subsidy of the churches, and the school question.

M. BASLY [Socialist, Paris] – Vote the abolition of the subsidy.

M. JULES FERRY – The associations, Messieurs, were about ten years ago one of the noisiest episodes in what you call the war of religion. From time to time public authorities have to defend themselves, and then ... (*'Hear, hear!' on the left. Ironic comments and noise on the right.*) people say they have declared war on religion. At a certain moment we had to enforce the laws of the state and insist that the religious congregations observe existing laws and decrees. (*'Hear, hear!' on the left. Interruptions on the right.*)

... There is, Messieurs, a second point, a second question which stirs up and heats debate and delays the establishment of religious peace in this country: the question of the state subsidy of the churches. On this matter my personal feelings are well known to everyone in this assembly. I support the state subsidy. I know very well that my honourable colleagues on this side [the extreme left] think that the abolition of the subsidy will better contribute to public peace.

If I believed that the separation of Church and State, the abolition of the subsidy, would serve public peace in this country, I would vote with them. (*Interruptions on the left.*) But I am profoundly convinced that far from pacifying religious disputes, this abolition would spread them into the tiniest village . . . (*'Hear, hear!' on the right. Interruptions on the extreme left.*) Messieurs, I have said nothing new and unexpected, and I would wish to be allowed to express myself freely . . . I believe that far from strengthening the state, the abolition of the subsidy would weaken it and strengthen only passions. (*'Hear, hear!' on various benches.*) . . . As for the lay schools, as for the separation of Church and school, I deny absolutely that, whether in law or in practice, it had the character of religious persecution which you attribute to it. (*Interruptions on the right and extreme left.*)

M. FERROUL [Radical-socialist, Aude] – You will be a cardinal before Jules Simon.

Speech of Jules Ferry to the Chamber of Deputies, 6 June 1889, in Jules Ferry, *Discours et Opinions*, vol. iv, Paris, 1896, pp. 475–8.

Boulangism

document 7

One way to discredit Boulanger was to tar him with the brush of Bonapartism; but in this speech, document (a), to an audience of Bonapartists, Boulanger proclaims his republicanism and his desire to open the Republic to those ejected beyond the pale of republican legitimacy. In his reply to Boulanger, document (b), Ferry wields the tar-brush again, and calls for republican unity against Boulanger. But he is anxious to win back radicals from Boulanger without conceding any of their criticisms of the parliamentary Republic.

(a) If I have attracted along with republican votes the votes of men who, in serving fallen regimes, also served the country, and those of electors who have remained faithful to names which, while they recall our misfortunes, recall also our glories, it is not because these men did me the injury of supposing that in spite of my republican protestations I wanted to restore one of the former regimes. It is rather that, instructed by experience, they are in agreement with me and, may I say also, with you, in wanting a new, national Republic, open to all honest men and to every progress made by the people, for the people, and in which the people would have not only the too frequently illusory right to express their wishes, but the power to realise them . . . If we are beginning our history again, it is to go back not to 1851, but rather to 1789.

Speech of Boulanger to the Bonapartist Committee of the Nièvre department, on 2 December 1888, anniversary of the *coup d'état* of Louis-Napoleon in 1851. Cited by Odile Rudelle, *La République absolue, 1870–1889*, Paris, 1982, p. 230.

(b) The innovators today are the most dismal and unsentimental of plagiarisers. The men of 1789 are asleep in their silent grave. Those beating at the door are the men of Brumaire! (*Prolonged applause. Agitation.*)

What is threatened is perhaps not immediately the republican form of government. The dynastic principle in this country seems to be played out. The head of the house of France believes in restoration by plebiscite (*Laughter*) and the Bonapartists are flowing to Boulangism like water to the river. (*Renewed laughter.*)

What is threatened is something higher and deeper: that is liberty itself, the government of the country by the country, government by Assemblies, everything for which France has striven for thirty years of parliamentary monarchy and for twenty years of Republic, everything that has been the passion of our youth and the dignity of our middle age. That is what is in danger! (*Unanimous approval.*)

. . . On the eve of the great Centenary, doubt enters our hearts. If this evil continues and triumphs, if the blow falls, Messieurs, we will in this year 1889 be witness to the greatest, most abject and colossal forswearing of all that France has sought, loved, adored and served for a hundred years! (*Renewed applause.*)

But, Messieurs, that will not be (*'No!' 'no!'*) if all republicans, united this time, radicals and moderates, understand that the origin of the [Boulangist] movement is not in a surge of new ideas and odd reforms; if they understand that the origin is elsewhere, in the lassitude of the nation, the need for peace and good government that France feels; if they understand that the duty of everyone, radical and moderate, is to work together for the restoration of the principles, traditions and practice of government in this country. (*Loud cheers.*)

. . . There are things we cannot do. We want the union of republicans, but we cannot and must not join together on the territory of the radicals. (*General agreement.*)

Can we accept revision?

I myself make very little distinction between the different shades of revisionist. There are those who want only to remove the prerogatives of the president of the Republic and the dignity of the Senate. I personally think that they are no different from those who want fairly and squarely to abolish the Senate and the presidency. (*'Hear, hear!'*)

Revision, besides, you see, Messieurs, by the logic of ideas and realities, is not just the abolition of the presidency and the Senate. It is worse than that: a Constituent Assembly. (*'Yes! yes!' 'Hear, hear!'*)

. . . In all kinds of folly the best thing is not to start at all. We are not revisionists, not in the least. We think that there is nothing which needs revision in the constitution at the moment. We will tell the electorate such, and we will stand before it against the revisionist party which draws together all the enemies of the constitutional Republic. (*Loud applause.*)

Speech by Jules Ferry to the Republican Association, 21 December 1888, in Jules Ferry, *Discours et Opinions*, vol. vi, Paris, 1898, pp. 126–8.

Revolution or reform?

document 8

These passages illustrate one element of the internal debate among socialists: how to achieve the socialist society. In document (a), the Marxist Jules Guesde, whose party has scored successes at recent municipal and parliamentary elections, is reluctant to shed the label of revolutionary socialism. Document (b) is part of a lengthy address to the court by the young anarchist Emile Henry after being sentenced to death; he was guillotined a month later. Document (c) is from a pamphlet by another anarchist, Fernand Pelloutier, who sees no purpose in individual acts of terrorism, but argues that if anarchists find working-class support and convert it into a revolutionary general strike, they can defeat the forces of the bourgeois state.

(a) Far from being mutually exclusive, electoral action and revolutionary action are complementary and have always been complementary in our country, where for all parties victorious insurrection has always followed and capped the vote.

Today socialism is legalist and electoralist in the same sense as all parties which have gone before and which are now combined against it with what strength they have left.

There is and will only be a single set of means to the end in view, which are determined by circumstance. Where a revolution is the end those means are always revolutionary. The ballot is revolutionary, however legal it may be, when it organises Labour against Capital and fights elections on the battleground of class. Parliamentary action is revolutionary, however party-political it may be, when its oratory rallies the discontented of the workshop and counter and when it demonstrates that capitalist society is opposed to them or powerless to satisfy them.

Riot on the other hand is anti-revolutionary and reactionary, despite its illegality and violence, because it affords moribund capitalism the popular blood-letting it needs to survive and postpones the hour of deliverance.

Jules Guesde in *Le Socialiste*, 10 November 1894, cited in Jacques Droz (ed.), *Le Socialisme démocratique, 1864–1960*, Armand Colin, 1966, p. 76.

(b) It was then [after the failure of the Carmaux miners' strike] that I decided . . . to add a voice that the bourgeois had heard before but believed had been silenced with Ravachol: that of dynamite.

I wanted to show the bourgeoisie that from now on it could have no unsullied pleasures, that its insolent victories would be undermined, that its golden calf would shake violently on its pedestal, until the final spasm which would topple it into slime and blood.

At the same time I wanted to show the miners that there was only one class of men, the anarchists, who felt for their suffering and were ready to avenge them. They had no seats in Parliament, like Monsieur Guesde and his consorts, yet they went to the guillotine.

. . . The bomb in the Café Terminus is the answer to your rape of liberty, your arrests, your house-searches, your press law, your mass expulsion of foreigners, your executions. But why, you ask, did I attack peaceful customers, who were listening to music, and were probably not magistrates, or deputies, or officials?

. . . Should we strike only the deputies who pass laws against us, the magistrates who enforce them and the police who arrest us?

I don't think so.

These men are only instruments who do not act in their own name; they are paid by the bourgeoisie for its own protection and are no more guilty than the rest.

The good bourgeois who have no official position but who cash their dividends and live idly on the profits created by the labour of workers should take their share of the reprisals.

And not only they but all those who are content with the existing order, who applaud the government's measures and are thus its accomplices, clerks on a salary of 300 to 500 francs a month who hate the people more than the rich bourgeois do, that stupid and conceited mass which sides always with the strongest, the usual clientele of the Terminus and other large cafés.

That is why I aimed into the crowd without choosing my victims.

Speech of Émile Henry at his trial, April 1894, in Jean Maitron, *Ravachol et les Anarchistes*, Collection Archives, Julliard, 1964, pp. 107, 109–10.

(c) SECOND WORKER: There would be the threat of revolt if not revolt itself everywhere at once. The government would have to freeze the garrisons. Instead of matching 30,000 insurgents with 100, 150 or 200,000 soldiers, in an area of about forty kilometres [25 miles] circumference, as in the classic revolution, the general strike would match 200,000 workers and 10,000 soldiers here, 10,000 and 500 there, or, as at Décazeville and Trignac, 1,000 or 1,200 against a brigade of gendarmerie. Can you see the difference? And look at the resources the strikers would have! Public transport would stop, street lights would go out, and it would be impossible to supply large centres . . .

FIRST WORKER: That is certainly an improvement over previous revolutions I hadn't been aware of before. But wouldn't the Paris garrison alone be enough to crush the insurgents, given the modern weapons available?

SECOND WORKER: Of course, if the insurgents were stupid enough to mass at two or three central points. But that is precisely what would have to be avoided, and what the strikers would avoid, having everything to lose. They would remain in their neighbourhoods and take control there first of small workshops and bakeries, then of larger workshops, and finally, but only after the victory, of big industrial establishments. One of two things would happen. Either the government would divide its forces between the neighbourhoods involved and whereas previously the mass of soldiers crushed small groups of insurgents now the mass of insurgents would crush small groups of soldiers. Or the government would confine its troops to barracks and await some isolated and imprudent action by the strikers. But if such a localised and central action did not take place and if the takeover of the workshops were undertaken by small groups of men who remained dispersed and elusive, and the army were immobilised, how long do you think the government could keep it fed?

FIRST WORKER: Three months, I reckon.

SECOND WORKER: Not a fortnight . . .

Fernand Pelloutier, 'Qu'est-ce que la grève générale?', cited in Jacques Julliard, *Fernand Pelloutier et les Origines du Syndicalisme d'Action Directe*, Seuil, 1971, pp. 326–7.

document 9

The *Ralliement*

The Ralliement *was an attempt by moderates on the Right to win the Opportunists away from the radicals in order to form a new majority based on the Centre Right and thus gain office. This is the thinking behind document (a), the manifesto of a new conservative republican party. However the Opportunists were reluctant to give any ground, and in document (b) the Prime Minister, Dupuy, brings out the spectre of the Right's intractable royalism in order to justify their monopoly of power.*

(a) Rest assured that we are no more now than then entering into open or covert conflict with the established regime. In our eyes the Republic is the legal government of the country. We have recognised it as such and we have no thought of retracting anything.

But there is a long way between recognising a government in principle and subscribing to the policies of the men in power.

Republican concentration has never been other than a war machine directed against conservative and liberal influences for the benefit of radicalism. It has had only one motto: 'clericalism, there is the enemy'; only one aim: the undisturbed appropriation of the Republic as private property; and only one method of government: the most intolerant exclusivism.

Our policy in view of uncertain but inevitable events has been to prepare the formation of a Tory Party bringing together as a constitutional opposition all those men of goodwill who are tired of the abuses and excesses of the party in power. The time had to come for the country . . . to try while avoiding crisis to form a truly national government which would remain faithful to the democratic currents of our time but resolve firmly to uphold the claims of authority, respect for beliefs and the regular enjoyment of liberty. Our intention was not to be taken by surprise when the hour came, and events prove that we were not lacking in foresight.

It is our task to organise the democratic conservative party with a sincere loyalty. All those who wish to check the apostles of socialist neo-radicalism and masonic sectarians – and they are legion – will take their place in its ranks.

We have no excessive demands, harbour no suspicion or bitterness, peddle no metaphysical theories or vain idealism. We must make haste, forget our quarrels and put forward a single platform in these words: *for an open, tolerant, and honest Republic.*

Jacques Piou, Manifesto of the *Droite républicaine*, in *Le Figaro*, 8 January 1893.

(b) I recognise that unlike their ancestors they have learned something. But they will be the first to agree with me that they have forgotten nothing, not even the way to the royalist committees where doubtless they are planning some parallel action, or even a convergent one. I accept that they will endure the Republic; I am asking whether they would defend it!

Speech of Charles Dupuy at Toulouse, 23 May 1893, in Maxime Lecomte, *Les Ralliés. Histoire d'un parti, 1886–1898*, Paris, 1898, p. 233.

document 10
Two views of Méline's ministry

Méline's government survived with the support of the Right, but the rules of republican legitimacy made it necessary for him to argue in document (a) that he was pursuing republican policies and held office by virtue of a truly republican majority. Not even someone as obviously conservative as Méline could admit to being on the Right. This hypocrisy is wittily exposed in document (b) by Anatole France, writing in 1901. The speaker, Henri Léon, vice-president of the royalist committees of the South-West, regrets the Méline era, when covertly if not openly, the Right was back in power.

(a) It is not enough to accuse a government of clericalism to demonstrate that it is clerical. You must prove it ... We are upholding the Concordat and the laws of state without being prejudiced or provocative, with a firm impartiality. (*'Hear, hear!'*) The only thing we refuse to do is to declare war on religion itself, because even if France is not clerical, it is for the most part extremely tolerant. We have a sincere respect for religion, something which annoys the party that sees religion as a relic of servitude only to be destroyed.

No, we are not governing with the Right. To govern with a party means to execute its policy, its manifesto, or part of it at least. Our enemies know as well as we do that our policy is republican, clearly republican, and we make no concessions to anyone on this. Besides, no one has been so insolent as to ask us to.

The Right votes with us because it prefers our policy to that which is leading from radicalism to collectivism and because it places the interest of the country before its dynastic preferences. Or rather it does not vote with us so much as against social revolution, which it has every right to do.

As for our majority, I claim that it is the true republican majority, and I refer those who daily challenge us to the many division lists which prove it. Knock away the votes of the Right and then do the same thing for the opposing minority by knocking away the support of the socialists. You will find that the majority of republicans is with us, and in the country that majority is even stronger. (*Loud applause.*)

I know that in the radical camp they have tried to undermine this calculation by calling all those who are not republicans of long standing monarchist, and excommunicating those called scathingly the *ralliés*, as if it were not permitted after twenty-seven years of Republic to open our ranks to sincere and loyal men, like our colleague the Count of Alsace, all of whose votes since the beginning of the parliament have been as republican as our own. I do not hesitate to say that such support is an honour for the government and gives it more strength than certain revolutionary collectivists whose names I don't need to mention. Suffice it to say that without the support of the pure socialists the radical party would be in a minority of republicans and because of that it will not and cannot break with them.

Speech of Méline to his constituents at Remiremont, 10 October 1897, in Georges Lachapelle, *Le Ministère Méline*, J. L. L. d'Artrey, Paris, 1928, pp. 118–21.

(b) With Méline we had everything. We, the royalists, were in charge of the government, the army, the judiciary, the administration, the police . . . Méline did us the immense service of giving us a reassuring air, of making us benign, benign, as benign as himself. He said that we were the republicans, and people believed him.

– With him, continued Henri Léon, we had everything, we were everything, we could do everything. We didn't even have to hide. We were not outside the Republic but above it. We dominated it from the heights of our patriotism. We were everyone who mattered, we were France. I am not soft on the whore [*la gueuse* – i.e. the Republic] but you have to admit she is sometimes good fun. Under Méline the police were exquisite, wonderful. Without exaggerating, they were wonderful. At a royalist demonstration which you kindly organised, Brécé, I shouted 'Up the police!' till I was hoarse. I meant it. The police were clouting the republicans smartly. Gérault-Richard was put in the cells for shouting: 'Long live the Republic!' Méline made life too easy for us. He was a real wet-nurse. He rocked us, he sent us to sleep . . . Happy times. Méline led the dance. Nationalists, monarchists, anti-Semites, plebiscitarians, we danced together to his village violin.

Anatole France, *M. Bergeret à Paris*, Calmann Levy, Livre de Poche, 1973, pp. 90–2.

document 11

Intellectuals in politics

Blum's recollections of the Dreyfus Affair, written nearly forty years after the event, when the rise of Fascism created the same sense of a minority embattled in defence of truth against the force of national self- deception, portrays the confident innocence of the 'Dreyfusards of the first hour'. They had evidence that the mole in the French military intelligence was not Dreyfus but one Major Esterhazy, and did not imagine that what they saw as the truth would be subordinated to the corporate interest of the army and to raison d'état.

With such a collection of documents and facts no trace of doubt remained in our minds. Our certainty was pure, whole and serious, and we were convinced that it would be shared spontaneously by the whole universe, once the universe was informed of what we had learned ourselves. This illusion must seem extraordinary today, after everything that happened, but it should seem natural if people try to put themselves in our place. The Dreyfusards have been accused of engineering a treacherous plot to divide France and tear it apart. But they did not and I think could not have suspected that there would be a Dreyfus Affair. For them everything was clear, luminous, obvious, and they did not doubt that universal reason must be persuaded by this truth. For the moment, at the end of the holidays [of 1897] public opinion was calm and indifferent; it was unaware and expected nothing. Yet when the truth was revealed what a generous cry would be heard throughout France! The nation had abhorred the crime as one, and as one it would proclaim the error and set it right! Three years before, people had wondered what punishments could chastise the traitor enough; now they would wonder what praises and rewards would even begin to rehabilitate the victim. Those who had had the misfortune to be closest concerned in the fateful proceedings, the judges of Dreyfus, his friends, his commanding officers, would be the first to make their confession and to express their remorse. We were enchanted by that prospect. The only painful, anxious feeling we had was one of impatience. For until he returned to France to be showered with flowers and good wishes, to be consoled by the commiseration of a whole country, the innocent was still far away, in chains on his torrid rock. He would be freed when the truth was made public, but when would that be? When would be the chosen moment? Feverishly we counted the days.

Léon Blum, *Souvenirs sur l'Affaire*, Gallimard, 1935, pp. 41–3.

document 12
J'accuse

Émile Zola's intervention was provoked by the clearing of Esterhazy by a military court, which left Dreyfus as guilty as ever. Zola's letter to the President of the Republic, published on 13 January 1898, is an indictment of military justice, the military hierarchy and the military mind, and alludes to the threat of a military coup d'état. *It betrays the same faith in the inevitable triumph of truth as the previous extract by Blum did.*

How could one military court be expected to overrule what another military court had done?

I am not even talking about the possible choice of judges. Isn't the higher notion of discipline which runs in the veins of these soldiers enough to invalidate their powers of equity? Discipline entails obedience. Do you expect a military court formally to contradict a minister of war, the great leader, when he has publicly proclaimed the finality of the court's decision to the applause of parliament? From a hierarchical point of view it is impossible.

An iniquitous verdict was returned [the acquittal of Esterhazy] which will always hang heavy on our military courts and cast a veil of suspicion over all their decisions. The first court [which condemned Dreyfus] might have been unintelligent, but the second [which acquitted Esterhazy] was necessarily criminal. Its excuse, I repeat, is that the supreme chief had spoken, proclaiming the verdict to be indefeasible, holy and above men, in such a way that no inferiors could contradict it. We are told about the honour of the army, and the need to love and respect it. Certainly, we have nothing but love and respect for the army which marches out at the first sign of danger, which would defend French soil, which is the whole people. But we are talking about another sort of army, upon whose dignity we are calling in our demand for justice. That army is the sabre, the dictator who may be forced upon us tomorrow. And God knows that I will not piously kiss the hilt of a sabre!

[There follows a series of accusations levelled against named officers of the military, from the Minister of War, General Mercier, downwards.] I do not know the people I am accusing, I have never seen them and I bear them neither bitterness nor hatred. For me they are only entities, spirits of evil-doing in society. My act today is nothing but a revolutionary means of hastening the explosion of justice and truth.

Emile Zola, *La Vérité en Marche*, Paris 1901, pp. 36–7, 93.

The Dreyfus Affair seen by nationalists

document 13

This extract is from a letter from the French commander at Fashoda, Marchand, to the cartoonist Forain. Forain had pictured him pensive under a tricolour, while in the foreground Kitchener was saying to a clergyman, 'How can I demoralise this good man?' and the reply came, 'I will have a go by reading him a few French papers.' Marchand had seen this cartoon in a

*newspaper given to him by the British. The message was that the campaign
of the Dreyfusards – the enemy within – undermined the morale of the army
and in the end made it unwilling to defend a fatherland which had sunk to
such depths.*

It was the 21 September, at Fashoda. For nearly ten months we
had had no news from France or Europe. Forty-eight hours
previously the Anglo-Egyptian army had arrived at Omdurman
and the Sirdar Kitchener was going to return to Khartoum.

On the orders of his commander and doubtless with honourable
intentions, Wingate left me a collection of English newspapers and
some French ones, *for which we had not dared ask*, but which we
accepted with gratitude. . .

I have only two lines to add. An hour after opening the French
papers the ten officers were shaking and crying. We learned that
the terrible Dreyfus Affair had been reopened by the horrible
campaign of those vile people. For thirty-six hours we were incap-
able of saying anything to each other. Such feelings cannot be
shared.

I have enlarged, exaggerated or changed nothing. On the
contrary.

I just want to tell you as I look at the last Forain cartoon of
October [1898] which has travelled 3,000 miles to get here, that
you must have a deep sense of proud patriotism. Otherwise you
could not draw as you do.

For that reason I ask permission to embrace you, if you will
permit me.

Major Marchand

Maurice Barrès, *Scènes et Doctrines du Nationalisme*, Paris, 1902,
pp. 371–2.

document 14

Faces of Radicalism

*These two extracts illustrate the difference between the claims and the actual
policies of the Radical party. Document (a) is an exposition by Camille
Pelletan of a broad agenda of reforms at the founding congress of the
Republican, Radical and Radical-Socialist Party. Document (b) is an inter-
pellation of the Combes government by Alexandre Millerand. He was*

chairman of a commission on social insurance, but was unable to obtain the support of the government for a pensions bill, partly because of the costs involved, partly because of its obsession with destroying the power of the Church.

(a) The first thought of the republican congress should be one of union against the common enemy. That thought must be the concern of all democrats defending themselves against open plots and schemes of *coup d'état.*

That thought has brought us together here though it extends far beyond these walls, for it rallies all the sons of the Revolution, whatever their differences, against all partisans of counter-revolution, their numbers swollen by accomplices found in the ranks of our erstwhile friends.

The best way to defend the Republic is to make it more republican . . . Most of the reforms promised still await enactment. Their time should have come long ago, and we can delay no longer. First come the reforms concerning clericalism. The law against teaching congregations is on the statute book. The country expects it to be enforced without weakness. If necessary it will require it. The struggle is on, and we must fight to the end . . . No one can consider the pact forged against liberty between the Papacy and the renascent Napoleonic dictatorship to be a republican institution. However we should not air our differences on this until the time has come to dissolve it: universal suffrage will decide.

Another danger is growing daily in all countries. That is the power that the concentration and handling of large capital is giving to high finance. We must protect the general interest of the country and the liberty and prosperity of all from its growing domination both by legislation against speculation and laws to nationalise certain monopolies and public services as the interests of national defence and agricultural and industrial production demand it.

Among the most pressing concerns in modern societies are social reforms. What divides us from the socialists is our passionate commitment to the principle of private property, the abolition of which we cannot even begin to contemplate. But precisely because this principle rests entirely on the inviolable right of each person to the fruit of his labour, we will defer to no one when it comes to introducing old-age pensions in a practicable way, to preventing large-scale industry from becoming a new feudalism, and to

speeding up the peaceful process which will make workers owners
of their tools and ensure the just remuneration of their labour.

Fiscal reforms are no less urgent. Our tax system weighs lightly
on the rich and heavily on the poor, especially on the mass of peasants who form the majority and the strength of the country. We
desire a progressive income tax which will lighten the burden on
workers and particularly on villages. We want a general overhaul
of the old system, especially a reform of the land tax and taxes
which tie up rural property.

Add to this equality of military service, reduced to two years.

That is the outline of our programme.

A declaration of Radical principles and policies by Camille
Pelletan at the founding congress of 1901, cited by Jean-Thomas
Nordmann, *La France Radicale*, 'Archives', Gallimard Julliard,
Paris, 1977, pp. 44–6.

(b) I come to this desk to demand an explanation from the president of the council – and this is something which concerns the
general policy of the government to the highest degree – of an
attitude which is in formal contradiction with the promises made
by the cabinet and which is preventing the commission [on social
insurance] from making any headway.

. . . I could never have imagined that any government could
limit the horizon of its ambitions to the struggle against the
religious congregations. (*'Hear, hear!' on several benches on the left and
centre.*)

What assures a place apart in the history of the republican party
and the gratitude of the people for the author of the law of 1901
[Waldeck-Rousseau] is that he is also the author of the law of 1884
[on trade union rights] and that at no time, even at the most
critical moments, did he as head of the government of 1899
separate social policy from republican defence.

In fact the sharper the struggle with the forces of the past, the
heavier the obligation on republican government to give the same
drive and passion to building the new world so impatiently awaited
as it does to the necessary task of pulling down the old one.

No one is more conscious than I of the fearful difficulties posed
by a pensions bill. But precisely because the task is difficult and
complex the republican party must pursue it with a tireless resolution, without being distracted from its goal. It will be assured that
far from weakening it, this fight for justice and the improvement

of the lot of the workers will give the party incomparable strength and credit in its daily battle with the enemies of the Republic, whether they show their faces or not.

Alexandre Millerand in the Chamber of Deputies, 17 March 1904, *Journal Officiel. Débats parlementaires. Chambre des Députés*, January–March 1904, p. 786.

document 15
Revolution as myth and reality

The Radical party was committed to the ideology of Revolution, but felt rather differently when public order was at stake. The death of a demonstrator during the Seine labourers' strike of 1908 provoked a massive political crisis which exposed the paradoxes of the Radical position. In document (a), Clemenceau, the President of the Council of Ministers, defends the policy of his government in the Chamber of Deputies against attack from the Left. In document (b), Jaurès continues the attack in the socialist daily, L'Humanité.

(a) M. THE PRESIDENT OF THE COUNCIL [Clemenceau]: You said that I was the enemy of socialism and of the working class. I reply: you do not represent socialism or the working class. I am a French citizen placed by chance in a difficult position . . . the responsibility of which I feel more keenly than others, as I should. You thought that you could frighten the government with verbal and physical violence. Well, the government is not frightened. (*Applause on the left and centre.*) That is its crime! It is not your enemy; it is not the workers' enemy and I have said as much. Its only enemies are those who break the law . . .

M. PAUL CONSTANS: Like the gendarmes.

M. THE PRESIDENT OF THE COUNCIL: because it has to ensure that the law is observed . . .

You will never find a government which allows anarchy to take a hold in this country, smashing cars, clubbing people, throwing stones at miners at work in the pit.

M. JAURES: You are anarchy crowned. (*'Hear, hear!' on the extreme left.*)

M. THE PRESIDENT OF THE COUNCIL: Fine. A nice piece of rhetoric. I am anarchist because I enforce the right to work. I am anarchist because I won't tolerate navvies being thrown into the Seine. I am anarchist because I won't permit houses to be set on fire. I am anarchist because I won't allow people to be beaten up with clubs. That is where we differ.

You see that in this motion something quite other than the Draveil-Vigneux incident is at stake ... a dead body is being exploited to attack the government and you say that we are responsible for this policy ...

M. EDOUARD VAILLANT: It's your policy which puts guns into the hands of gendarmes.

M. THE PRESIDENT OF THE COUNCIL: Messieurs, I have finished. The government cannot be held in the least responsible for events it is the first to deplore (*Exclamations on the extreme left*), as I said to begin with.

Such things have happened under all governments, they are unavoidable. Our duty is the same as that of all previous governments – to uphold justice – and that we shall do.

The House will declare whether it condemns this anarchy, or whether it thinks that for the good of the future social revolution we must grapple with revolutionaries who want only disorder and violence. It will declare whether it wants to help us establish a legal order which opens the way to reform in order to prevent revolution. That is the policy that the government is proposing. (*Loud applause on a large number of benches.*)

Speech of Clemenceau in the Chamber of Deputies, 11 June 1908. *Journal Officiel. Débats parlementaires. Chambre des Députés*, January–July 1908, pp. 1166–7.

(b) M. Clemenceau made a moving case for the murderous gendarmes of Draveil, and the Chamber gave him authority to use the appropriate repressive measures ... M. Clemenceau declared that we alone were responsible and alone ought to be court-martialled. The murderers will be summoned only to be congratulated, because they have fought the good fight against 'the Revolution' denounced yesterday by M. Clemenceau. This evocation of the revolutionary peril by all governments as they slide inevitably towards reaction is a miserable comedy. Méline performed it, [Casimir-]Périer too, perhaps with less vulgarity than the current president of the council. Those Radicals who have now decided to follow conservative policies to the bitter end were right yesterday to support M. Clemenceau ... Socialism will be isolated, exposed to many attacks, and buffeted by winds from every horizon. But democracy which seems to have lost its way will one day advance to meet it.

A massive conservative coalition is now forming against us, against the proletariat. M. Clemenceau has never been other than a negative force and was predestined to this negative action. He succeeded in upsetting the republican and democratic victory of 1906. But he will not break the strength of the working class and socialism. They will organise with an energy renewed by the trials they have endured, and with a force and faith only increased by the universal unleashing of blind hatred.

Article by Jean Jaurès in *L'Humanité*, 12 June 1908.

War and revolution

document 16

The Paris Commune was as much patriotic as revolutionary. Here the military governor of Paris, General Trochu, describes the series of coups against the incompetent provisional government which culminated in the insurrection of 18 March 1871. Trochu was removed from his post in an attempt to placate the angry Parisians after the defeat of Buzenval on 19 January 1871, but to no avail.

I have placed before you a sort of history of the Paris sectarians during the siege. I have demonstrated that each of their assaults on public order coincided with one of our [military] disasters, as if they wanted to complete them and exploit them: on 8 October, after the surrender of Strasbourg; on 31 October, after the surrender of Metz; on 22 January, after the battle of Buzenval . . . All the assaults were planned and executed in a spirit of violence: hatred of the government and a feeling that the Government of National Defence was betraying the country because it did not order a mass mobilisation. They demanded war to the death and insisted that they they would have it, with or without the government. In the same spirit they seized the cannon which had been placed on the Place de Wagram and carried them to Montmartre, where the bastion of the insurrection was erected.

Testimony of General Trochu to the National Assembly, 15 June 1871, *Journal Officiel*, 16 June 1871, p. 1379.

document 17

Two views of Colonialism

*France's colonial policy was controversial. For some it represented the pros-
pect of recovering some form of national greatness without antagonising
Germany. For others the very supine position before Germany which that
strategy entailed was enough to condemn it. The question was made more
bitter by party-political disputes. Colonies were initially the policy of the
Opportunist republicans, particularly of Jules Ferry, whose praises are sung
in document (a) by Charles Freycinet (whose work was first published in
1913). But colonial adventures were disliked by the Radicals, often supported
by the Right. In document (b) Clemenceau voices his hostility to the Tonkin
expedition in a debate which finished off the Ferry ministry.*

(a) M. Jules Ferry must be congratulated for understanding how
much France suffered from the loss of its colonial empire. The
acquisition of Algeria and even of Tunisia did not end the regrets
caused by the loss of so many glorious possessions in Asia and
Africa in the eighteenth century. These regrets had become even
sharper after the disastrous war of 1871. France felt diminished
both in territory and in glory. Direct revenge was impossible, but
she wanted at least to deploy her armed forces, to show that they
were still strong. Compensation could not be found close by, so it
was sought far off. Inevitably she was going to move into other
parts of the world, imitating in this respect most of the other great
European nations. M. Jules Ferry appreciated this mentality and,
without positively planning the founding of a colonial empire, he
exploited opportunities which arose to achieve it. The enterprise
was not illusory, and the shock waves are still being felt. The Asian
epic was followed by the African epic. After Annam and Tonkin
France directed her energies to the Sudan, the Congo and Dahomey.
As if these territories were not enough to absorb her energies,
France is today staking a claim to Morocco, in spite of difficulties,
even dangers, of which she is not unaware. Though mistakes have
been made, M. Jules Ferry has the good fortune to remain the
initiator of our twentieth-century colonial expansion.

Charles de Freycinet, *Souvenirs, 1878–1893*, Da Capo Press, New York,
1973, pp. 268–9.

(b) Messieurs, Prince Bismarck is a dangerous enemy; he is
perhaps even more dangerous as a friend. Yes! it was he who

dangled Tunis in front of you at the Congress of Berlin; he who put you at loggerheads with England as I said just now; he who is negotiating with you about the Congo at the conference table of Berlin. And while we are wasting our money and the best of our blood in crazy enterprises, he is waging a terrible economic war against us, and patiently awaiting his fee for services rendered.

Perhaps he has done us more harm in peace than in war. In war there was the feeling that we had to pull together to repel the invader; after the defeat there was the common sentiment of recovery by means of work, single-mindedness and sacrifice. The dignity of the defeated was intact because thanks to the efforts of the republican party right remained on our side. (*Applause on the extreme left.*)

Since the war both governments and governed have been affected by anxiety about the future, by a sense of instability and the feeling that the whole edifice of peace depends on the caprice of one man, by the temptations of a pacific policy and the bad example of those who turn for security to power and force. Nervous irritation, divisions, powerlessness, and a growing appetite for territory has followed. Since our neighbour has taken something, so should we. Moral uprightness has been weakened, rights sacrificed, and national policy perverted. (*'Hear, hear!' and loud applause on the extreme left.*)

Without realising it or having reflected for a single moment, we have compromised what we should have safeguarded above all else, namely national dignity, independence and honour. (*Renewed applause on the extreme left.*)

I am no longer speaking of the past. I want to forget it. If I establish that there is an immediate, pressing interest not only from the financial point of view, but also from the point of view of our policy in Europe, concerning what remains and can remain of our dignity among the countries of Europe; if I can establish that there is still time to change our policy, that we can stop these colonial expeditions which take our gold and the best of our blood by killing the flower of our army, then you must take a decision which involves much more than the Tonkin expedition.

I know full well that we will take Tonkin. I know that our gallant soldiers will defeat the Chinese wherever they confront them. I don't doubt it, and no one ever has doubted it. But the question at the moment is not Tonkin but something higher. The question is France. (*Loud applause on the extreme left and right.*)

Speech of Clemenceau to the Chamber of Deputies, in *Journal Officiel. Débats parlementaires. Chambre des Députés*, 28 November 1884, p. 1501.

Can a Republic be great?

document 18

For the royalist Charles Maurras, Republic and greatness were mutually exclusive terms. In this piece, written in the aftermath of Fashoda and the Dreyfus Affair, Maurras turns for evidence to the reflections of Ernest Renan after 1870, and takes a few liberties with French history. Maurras died in 1952.

Renan wrote these words: 'The day France cut her king's head off, she committed suicide.'

Louis XIV bequeathed France an army and a navy. The restoration [of 1815] left her a magnificent position in Europe. Louis-Philippe left the military organisation created by the law of 1832, by which I mean the troops who won the Crimean War. Such was the work of the House of France in its last moments. The dynasty succumbed and from that time we have been falling. Castastrophes unknown since the fifteenth century (except that in the fifteenth century the national dynasty pulled itself together and the country with it) have repeatedly exhausted us. What are Pavia and Rossbach, so often mentioned, when compared to Sedan and Waterloo? Revolutions have succeeded revolutions. The state is bankrupt. Three times foreigners have invaded Paris. We have had two civil wars. We have witnessed Italian unification, German unification, and the outrageous growth of the double Anglo-Saxon Empire.

Never has political France been so small. Since then she has achieved a masterpiece of littleness: she has made herself a Republic, which means she has decided to be weak and defeated. Renan warned us about it. 'There are some,' he said, 'who imagine a powerful, influential, glorious Republic. Let them think again and choose. Of course the Republic is possible in France, but a Republic scarcely more important than the Swiss Republic – and less respected. The Republic can have neither army nor diplomacy; the Republic would be a singularly useless military state, with extremely poor discipline. The basis of a Republic is election, and a republican society is as weak as a military unit which elects its officers. The fear of not being re-elected paralyses all energy.'

Energy. Our deputies may well show some for an immediate interest, which arrests the eye, which the crowd sees and applauds. They have no energy for a future interest, however grave it might be. They reckon with 1902 and 1906 [dates of elections], but not with 1950. 1950 could not be further from their thoughts. Living Frenchmen with the vote are their only concern.

What this country is lacking is an instrument of foresight in the central government. What it lacks, to be truthful, is a future.

Charles Maurras, *Une Campagne royaliste au 'Figaro', 1901–2*, Nouvelle Imprimerie Nationale, 1925, pp. 496–7.

Socialism and revolution
document 19

The achievement of Jaurès was to reconcile the commitment of the French working class to the cause of international socialism and a commitment to the defence of the fatherland. This he did by reference to the revolutionary-patriotic tradition of 1792, in which France, the patrie, *or land of liberty, was defended by volunteer forces against Austrian and Prussian armies. These volunteers then went on to liberate oppressed peoples. The defence of France was thus equated with the defence of liberty and civilisation on behalf of humanity. This is the burden of the speech of the trade union leader, Jouhaux, at the graveside of the murdered Jaurès in 1914.*

Jaurès consoled us in our passionate drive for peace. It is neither his fault nor ours if peace has not prevailed. Before we march off to the great massacre, in the name of those workers who have already left, in the name of those who are about to leave, including myself, I proclaim before this coffin our hatred of the imperialism and savage militarism which have unleashed this horrible crime.

. . . If he were still here, if a cowardly assassin had not stifled his voice for ever, he would tell us, comrades, that you will be defending not just the national cause but the cause of the International and that of civilisation, the cradle of which is France.

. . . Caught up in the struggle, we will rise to repel the invader, to safeguard the patrimony of civilisation and generous ideology bequeathed to us by history. We do not wish those few liberties we snatched with such difficulty from evil forces to be lost. Our wish has always been to enlarge popular rights, and to widen the field of liberties. It is because of this wish that we answer 'present' to the mobilisation order. We will never fight a war of conquest.

... The working class remembers that it has always been nourished by revolutionary traditions of the soldiers of the Year II who took liberty to the world, that it must not arm in hatred of a people and that it must not direct its anger against a nation which is itself a victim of despots and bad leaders.

Emperors of Germany and Austria-Hungary, Prussian Junkers and great Austrian lords who have sought war out of hatred for democracy, we swear to ring the knell of your regimes.

We will be the soldiers of liberty who create freedom for the oppressed and harmony between nations through mutual understanding and an alliance of peoples. With this ideal we will conquer.

Yes, Jaurès, your everlasting memory will guide us in the terrible conflict which is beginning. It will stand before us like a flame that the torment will not extinguish. And before I go to meet the danger, I will proclaim aloud our indestructible faith in the International, and our resolution to secure every liberty by bitter struggle for those who await them in hope.

No, comrades, our ideal of human reconciliation and happiness in society will not fade. It has been checked, but even so better conditions to spread it around the world are being prepared.

The shadow of the great Jaurès bears witness to this.

Speech of Léon Jouhaux at the funeral of Jean Jaurès, 4 August 1914, in Jean Rabaut, *L'Antimilitarisme français*, Paris, 1975, pp. 104–7.

Bibliography

WHICH REPUBLIC?

General accounts
1 Robert Anderson, *France, 1870–1914*, Routledge and Kegan Paul, 1977.
2 Gordon Wright, *France in Modern Times*, Murray, 3rd edition, 1981.
3 Jean-Marie Mayeur and Madeleine Rebérioux, *The Third Republic from its Origins to 1914*, Cambridge University Press, 1984. This is a translation of *Les Débuts de la Troisième République*, Seuil, 1973 and *La République radicale?*, Seuil, 1975.
4 Roger Magraw, *France 1815–1914. The Bourgeois Century*, Fontana, 1983.
5 Theodore Zeldin, *France, 1848–1945*, 2 vols. Oxford University Press, 1973 and 1977.

The foundation of the Republic
6 Louis M. Greenberg, *Sisters of Liberty. Marseille, Lyon, Paris and the Reaction to the Centralized State, 1868–1871*, Harvard University Press, 1971.
7 Michael Howard, *The Franco-Prussian War*, Rupert Hart-Davis, 1968.
8 J. P. T. Bury, *Gambetta and the National Defence*, Longman, 1936.
9 J. P. T. Bury and Robert Tombs, *Thiers, 1797–1877. A Political Biography*, Allen and Unwin, 1986.
10 Robert Tombs, *The War against Paris, 1871*, Cambridge University Press, 1981.
11 Samuel Osgood, *French Royalism since 1870*, Martinus Nijhoff, The Hague, 1970.
12 Robert Locke, *French Legitimists and the Politics of Moral Order in the Early Third Republic*, Princeton University Press, 1974.
13 J. P. T. Bury, *Gambetta and the Making of the Third Republic*, Longman, 1973.

14 Jean-Claude Wartelle, 'L'Election Barodet, avril 1873', *Revue d'Histoire Moderne et Contemporaine*, 27, 1980, pp. 600–30.

15 John Rothney, *Bonapartism after Sedan*, Cornell University Press, 1969.

16 Philip A. Bertocci, *Jules Simon. Republican Anticlericalism and Cultural Politics in France, 1848–1886*, University of Missouri Press, 1978.

17 Odile Rudelle, *La République Absolue. Aux origines de l'instabilité ministérielle de la France contemporaine, 1870–1889*, Sorbonne, 1982.

THE REPUBLIC OF THE NOTABLES

18 Leslie Derfler, *President and Parliament. A Short History of the French Presidency*, Florida University Press, 1983.

19 J. P. T. Bury, *Gambetta's Final Years, 1877–1882*, Longman, 1982.

20 Jean Estèbe, *Les Ministres de la République, 1871–1914*, Fondation Nationale des Sciences Politiques, 1982.

21 Daniel Salem, 'Le Sénat 'conservateur' de la Troisième République', *Revue d'Histoire Economique et Sociale*, 50, 1972, pp. 518–50.

22 Mattei Dogan, 'Les Filières de la carrière politique en France', *Revue française de Sociologie*, 8, 1967, pp. 468–92.

23 Mattei Dogan, 'La Stabilité du personnel parlementaire sous la Troisième République', *Revue française de Science Politique*, 3, 1953, pp. 319–348.

24 Pierre Guiral and Guy Thuillier, *La Vie Quotidienne des Députés en France de 1871 à 1914*, Hachette, 1980.

24a Robert de Jouvenel, *La République des Camarades*, 1914, Grasset, 1934, p. 17.

25 Alexandre Pilenco, *Les Mœurs du Suffrage Universel en France, 1848–1928*, Revue Mondiale, 1930.

26 Roger Thabault, *Education and Change in a Rural Community. Mazières-en-Gâtine, 1848–1914*, Routledge and Kegan Paul, 1971.

27 Robert Gildea, *Education in Provincial France. A Study of Three Departments*, Oxford, Clarendon Press, 1983.

LEFT AND RIGHT

28 Patrick K. Bidelman, *Pariahs stand up! The Founding of the Liberal Feminist Movement in France, 1858–1889*, Westport, Connecticut, 1982.

119

29   Jean T. Joughin, *The Paris Commune and French Politics, 1871–1880*, Johns Hopkins University Press, 1955.

30   Sanford Elwitt, *The Making of the Third Republic. Class and Politics in France, 1868–1884*, Louisiana State University Press, 1975.

31   Michael S. Smith, 'Free trade and protection in the early Third Republic', *French Historical Studies*, 10, 1977, pp. 293–314.

32   Charles-Robert Ageron, *L'Anticolonialisme en France de 1871 à 1914*, Presses Universitaires de France, 1973.

33   Peter Rutkoff, *Revanche and Revision. The Ligue des Patriotes and the Origin of the Political Right in France, 1882–1900*, Ohio University Press, 1981.

34   David Watson, *Georges Clemenceau. A Political Biography*, Eyre Methuen, 1974.

35   Pierre Barral, *Les Agrariens français de Méline à Pisani*, Cahiers de la Fondation Nationale des Sciences Politiques, 1968.

36   Benjamin Martin, *Count Albert de Mun, Paladin of the Third Republic*, Chapel Hill, University of North Carolina, 1978.

37   Jean el Gammal, 'Un Pré-Ralliement: Raoul-Duval et la Droite républicaine, 1885–1887', *Revue d'Histoire Moderne et Contemporaine*, 29, 1982, pp. 599–621.

38   Adren Dansette, *L'Affaire Wilson et la Chute du Président Grévy*, Perrin, 1936.

39   Frederic H. Seager, *The Boulanger Affair*, Cornell University Press, 1969.

40   Mermeix, *Les Coulisses du Boulangisme*, Cerf, 1890.

41   Jacques Néré, 'Les Elections de Boulanger dans le département du Nord', complementary thesis, Paris, 1959.

SOCIAL STRUCTURE

42   Eugen Weber, *Peasants into Frenchmen. The Modernization of Rural France, 1870–1914*, Chatto and Windus, 1977.

43   Pierre Barral in Fernand Braudel and Ernest Labrousse, *Histoire économique et sociale de la France*, 4:i, Presses Universitaires de France, 1979.

44   Georges Duby and Armand Wallon (eds.), *Histoire de la France rurale*, Vol. 3, Seuil, 1976.

45   Leo Loubere, *The Red and the White*, Albany, 1978.

46   Philippe Gratton, *La Lutte des Classes dans les Campagnes*, Editions Anthropos, 1971.

47 Emile Guillaumin, *Six Ans de Lutte Syndicale*, Editions des Cahiers Bourbonnais, Moulins, 1977.

48 Suzanne Berger, *Peasants against Politics. Rural Organization in Brittany, 1911–1967*, Harvard University Press, 1972.

49 Yves Lequin, 'Labour in the French Economy since the Revolution', *Cambridge Economic History*, VII, Cambridge University Press, 1978.

50 Madeleine Guilbert, *Les Fonctions de la Femme dans l'Industrie*, Mouton, Paris-The Hague, 1966.

51 Patricia Hilden, *Working Women and Socialist Politics in France, 1880–1914. A Regional Study*, Clarendon Press, Oxford, 1986.

52 Rolande Trempé, *Les Mineurs de Carmaux, 1848–1914*, 2 vols., Editions Ouvrières, 1971.

53 Michael P. Hanagan, *The Logic of Solidarity. Artisans and Industrial Workers in Three French Towns*, University of Illinois Press, 1980.

54 Leonard Berlanstein, *The Working People of Paris, 1871–1914*, Johns Hopkins University Press, 1984.

55 Michelle Perrot, *Workers on Strike. France 1871–1890*, Berg, 1987.

56 F. F. Ridley, *Revolutionary Syndicalism in France*, Cambridge University Press, 1970.

57 Madeleine Guilbert, *Les Femmes et l'Organisation syndicale avant 1914*, Centre National de Recherche Scientifique, Paris, 1966.

58 Joel Michel, 'Syndicalisme minier et politique dans Nord/Pas-de-Calais: le cas Basly, 1880–1914', *Le Mouvement Social*, 87, 1974, pp. 9–33.

59 Peter Schöttler, *Naissance des Bourses du Travail*, Presses Universitaires de France, 1985.

60 Christian Baudelot, Roger Establet, Jacques Malemort, *La Petite Bourgeoisie en France*, Maspéro, 1974.

61 Françoise Raison-Jourde, *La Colonie auvergnate de Paris au XIXe siècle*, Commission des Travaux Historiques, Paris, 1976.

62 Alain Faure, 'L'Épicerie parisienne au XIXe siècle ou la corporation éclatée', *Le Mouvement Social*, 108, 1979, pp. 113–30.

63 Karen Offen, 'The Second Sex and the baccalauréat in republican France, 1880–1924', *French Historical Studies*, 13, 1983, pp. 252–86.

64 George Weisz, *The Emergence of Modern Universities in France, 1863–1914*, Princeton University Press, 1983.

65 Christophe Charle, *Les Hauts Fonctionnaires en France au XIXe siècle*, 'Archives', Gallimard Julliard, 1986.

66 Henry Bérenger, *Les Prolétaires intellectuels en France*, La Revue, Paris, 1901.

67 Maurice Lévy-Leboyer, 'Le Patronat français a-t-il été malthusien?' *Le Mouvement Social*, 88, 1974, pp. 3–49.

68 Maurice Lévy-Leboyer, 'The large corporation in France', in A. D. Chandler and H. Daems (eds.), *Managerial Hierarchies*, Harvard University Press, 1980.

SOCIALISM

69 Madeleine Rebérioux, 'Le Socialisme français', in J. Droz (ed.), *Histoire générale du Socialisme*, Presses Universitaires de France, 1974.

69a Peter Schöttler, 'Politique syndicale ou lutte des classes: notes sur le syndicalisme apolitique des Bourses du Travail'. *Le Mouvement Social*, 116, 1981, pp. 16–17.

70 Claude Willard, *Le Mouvement socialiste en France, 1893–1905: les Guesdistes*, Editions Sociales, 1965.

71 David Stafford, *From Anarchism to Reformism*, Weidenfeld and Nicholson, 1971.

72 Pierre Sorlin, *Waldeck-Rousseau*, Armand Colin, 1966.

72a Maurice Charnay, *Les Allemanists*, M. Rivière, 1912, p. 45.

73 Michel Winock, 'La scission de Châtellerault et la naissance du Parti allemaniste', *Le Mouvement Social* 75, 1971, pp. 33–62.

74 Jacques Julliard, *Fernand Pelloutier et les Origines du Syndicalisme d'Action Directe*, Seuil, 1971.

75 Patrick Hutton, *The Cult of the Revolutionary Tradition: the Blanquists in French Politics, 1864–1893*, University of California Press; 1981.

76 Joan Scott, 'French socialist municipalities in the 1890s', *Le Mouvement Social*, 111, 1980.

77 James Joll, *The Anarchists*, Eyre and Spottiswoode, 1964, 2nd ed., 1979.

78 Jean Maitron, *Le Mouvement anarchiste en France*, I, Maspéro, 1975.

79 Madeleine Rebérioux, 'Le Mur des Fédérés', in Pierre Nora, *Les Lieux de Mémoire. I. La République*, Gallimard. Nouvelle Revue Française, 1984, pp. 619–49.

80 Charles Sowerwine, *Sisters or Citizens? Women and Socialism in France since 1876*, Cambridge University Press, 1982.

81 Carl Landauer, 'The Origins of socialist Reformism in France', *International Review of Social History*, 12, 1967, pp. 81–107.

82 Robert P. Baker, 'Socialism in the Nord, 1880–1914', *International Review of Social History*, 12, 1967, 357–89.

83 Simone Derruo-Boniol, 'Le Socialisme dans l'Allier de 1848 à 1914', *Cahiers d'Histoire*, 2, 1957, pp. 115–61.

84 Tony Judt, *Socialism in Provence, 1871–1914*, Cambridge University Press, 1979, argues instead that the adoption of socialism by the peasants of the Var represented a break with the past and with the Radical middle class.

85 Harvey Goldberg, *Life of Jean Jaurès*, University of Wisconsin Press, 1962.

86 Leslie Derfler, *Alexandre Millerand. The Socialist Years*, Mouton, Paris-The Hague, 1977.

THE CONSOLIDATION OF THE ELITE

87 Michael S. Smith, *Tariff Reform in France, 1860–1900. The Politics of Economic Interest*, Cornell University Press, 1980.

88 Alexander Sedgwick, *The Ralliement in French Politics, 1890–98*, Harvard University Press, 1965.

89 J. Dean O'Donnell, *Lavigerie in Tunisia, 1875–1892*, University of Georgia Press, 1979.

89a Maxime Lecomte, *Les Ralliés. Histoire d'un parti, 1886–1898*, Flammarion, 1898, p. 179.

90 Alain Bonnefous, 'Les Royalistes du Nord et le Ralliement', *Revue du Nord*, xlvii, no. 184, 1965, pp. 29–48.

91 Zeev Sternhell, 'National Socialism and Anti-Semitism: the case of Maurice Barrès', *Journal of Contemporary History*, vol. 8, no. 4, 1973, pp. 47–66.

92 Jean Bouvier, *Les Deux Scandales de Panama*, 'Archives', Gallimard Julliard, 1964.

93 Zeev Sternhell, *La Droite Révolutionaire, 1885–1914. Les Origines Françaises du Fascisme*, Seuil, 1978.

94 Stephen Wilson, *Ideology and Experience. Antisemitism in France at the Time of the Dreyfus Affair*, Fairleigh Dickinson University Press and Associated University Press, 1982.

95 Rosemonde Sanson, 'La Fête de Jeanne d'Arc en 1894. Controverse et célébration', *Revue d'Histoire Moderne et Contemporaine*, 20, 1973, pp. 444–63.

Bibliography

96   John A. Scott, *Republican Ideas and the Liberal Tradition in France, 1870–1914*, Columbia University Press, 1951.

97   J. E. S. Haywood, 'The Official Social Philosophy of the Third Republic: Léon Bourgeois and Solidarism', *International Review of Social History*, 6, 1961, pp. 19–48.

98   Marcel Ruby, *Le Solidarisme*, Librairie Gedalge, 1971.

99   William Burridge, *Destiny Africa. Cardinal Lavigerie and the Making of the White Fathers*, G. Chapman, 1966.

100 Henri Brunschwig, *French Colonialism, 1871–1914. Myth and Reality*, Pall Mall Press, 1966.

101 C. M. Andrew and A. J. Kanya-Forstner, 'The French "colonial party": its composition, aims and influence, 1885–1914', *Historical Journal*, xiv, 1971, pp. 99–128.

102 Darrell Bates, *The Fashoda Incident of 1898*, Oxford University Press, 1984.

THE DREYFUS AFFAIR

103 Douglas Johnson, *France and the Dreyfus Affair*, Blandford Press, 1966.

104 H. R. Kedward, *The Dreyfus Affair*, Longman, 1969.

105 Jean-Denis Bredin, *The Affair. The Case of Alfred Dreyfus*, Sidgwick and Jackson, 1987.

105a Charles Péguy, *Notre Jeunesse*, 1910, Gallimard, 1957, pp. 213–14.

105b Bernard-Lazare, *Contre l'Antisémitisme*, Stock, 1896, p. 32.

105c Maurice Barrès, *Scènes et Doctrines du Nationalisme*, Juven, 1902, p. 152.

106 Michael Marrus, *The Politics of Assimilation. A Study of the French Jewish Community at the Time of the Dreyfus Affair*, Oxford University Press, 1971.

107 Cécile Delhorbe, *L'Affaire Dreyfus et les Ecrivains français*, Neuchâtel-Paris, 1932.

108 Géraldi Leroy (ed.), *Les Ecrivains et l'Affaire Dreyfus*, Presses Universitaires de France, 1983.

109 Pascal Ory and Jean-François Sirinelli, *Les Intellectuels en France de l'Affaire Dreyfus à nos jours*, Armand Colin, 1986.

109a Emile Zola, *La Vérité en Marche*, E. Fasquelle, 1901, pp. 19, 93, 104, 126.

109b Anatole France, *L'Anneau d'Améthyste* (Calmann Lévy, 1899), p. 199.

109c L'Amitié Charles Péguy, *Feuillets Mensuels*, 22, July 1951, p. 5.

110 Robert J. Smith, *The Ecole Normale Supérieure and the Third Republic*, Albany, 1982.

111 Mildred J. Headings, *French Freemasonry under the Third Republic*, Johns Hopkins University Press, 1949.

112 Janine Ponty, 'La Presse quotidienne et l'affaire Dreyfus en 1898–9', *Revue d'Histoire Moderne et Contemporaine*, 21, 1974, pp. 193–220.

113 Roger Glenn Brown, *Fashoda Reconsidered. The Impact of Domestic Politics on French Policy in Africa, 1893–98*, Johns Hopkins University Press, 1969.

114 Eugen Weber, *Action Française. Royalism and reaction in Twentieth-Century France*, Stanford University Press, 1962, reprinted 1969.

115 Maurice Larkin, '"La République en danger"? The pretenders, the army and Déroulède, 1898–9', *English Historical Review*, 100, 1985, pp. 85–105.

116 Douglas Porch, *The March to the Marne. The French Army, 1871–1914*, Cambridge University Press, 1981.

RADICALISM

117 J. T. Nordmann, *Histoire des Radicaux, 1820–1973*, La Table Ronde, 1974.

118 J. T. Nordmann, *La France Radicale*, 'Archives', Gallimard Julliard, 1977.

119 Serge Berstein, *Histoire du Parti Radical*, I, Fondation Nationale des Sciences Politiques, 1980.

120 Benjamin Martin, 'The Creation of the Action Libérale Populaire', *French Historical Studies*, 9, 1976, pp. 660–89.

121 Henri Guillemin, *L'Arrière Pensée de Jaurès*, Gallimard, 1966.

122 R. A. Winnacker, 'The Délégation des Gauches', *Journal of Modern History*, 9, 1937, pp. 449–70.

123 Gérard Baal, 'Combes et la République des Comités', *Revue d'Histoire Moderne et Contemporaine*, 24, 1977, pp. 260–85.

124 Edward Shorter and Charles Tilly, *Strikes in France, 1830–1968*, Cambridge University Press, 1974.

125 Jacques Julliard, 'Jeune et vieux syndicat chez les mineurs du Pas-de-Calais', *Le Mouvement Social*, 47, 1964, pp. 7–30.

126 Charles Wormser, *La République de Clemenceau*, Presses Universitaires de France, 1961.

Bibliography

126a Andy Pitt, 'The Bourse du Travail of Saint-Etienne', unfinished London Ph.D thesis, cap. on the Bourse and politics, p. 27.

127 Charles K. Warner, *The Winegrowers of France and the Government since 1875*, Columbia University Press, 1960.

128 J. Harvey Smith, 'Agricultural workers and the French winegrowers revolt of 1907', *Past and Present*, 79, 1978.

129 Jacques Julliard, *Clemenceau, briseur de grèves*, 'Archives', Gallimard Julliard, 1965.

130 Bernard Georges and Denise Tintant, *Léon Jouhaux, cinquante ans de syndicalisme, I. Des Origines à 1921*, Presses Universitaires de France, 1962.

131 Judith Stone, *The Search for Social Peace: Reform Legislation in France, 1890–1914* State University, New York, 1985.

132 Steven Hause and Anne R. Kenney, *Women's Suffrage and Social Politics in the French Third Republic*, Princeton University Press, 1984.

133 Peter Shankland, *Death of an Editor*, Kimber, 1981.

NATIONALISM

134 Claude Digeon, *La Crise Allemande de la Pensée française, 1870–1914*, Presses Universitaires de France, 1959.

134a Georges Darien, *La Belle France*, 1900, 10/18, 1978, p. 44.

134b Léon Gambetta, speech of 26 June 1871, in *Discours*, vol. ii, Paris, 1881, p. 23.

135 J. M. Roberts, 'The Paris Commune from the Right', *English Historical Review*, 1973.

136 Karl Marx, *The Civil War in France*, International Working Men's Association, 1921.

137 Allan Mitchell, *The German Influence in France after 1870. The Formation of the French Republic*, Chapel Hill: University of North Carolina Press, 1979.

138 Jacques et Mona Ozouf, 'Le Thème du patriotisme dans les manuels primaires', *Le Mouvement Social*, 49, 1964, pp. 5–31. Reprinted in Mona Ozouf, *L'École de la France*, Gallimard, 1984.

139 Félix Ponteil, *La Méditerranée et les Puissances depuis l'ouverture jusqu'à la nationalisation du Canal de Suez*, Payot, 1964.

140 Winfried Baumgart, *Imperialism. The Idea and Reality of British and French Colonial Expansion, 1880–1914*, Oxford University Press, 1982.

141 François Bédarida, 'L'Armée et la République. Les opinions politiques des officiers français', *Revue Historique*, 232, 1964, pp. 119–164.

142 Raoul Girardet, *La Société militaire dans la France contemporaine, 1815–1939*, Plon, 1953.

143 Richard D. Challener, *The French Theory of the Nation in Arms, 1866–1939*, New York, Columbia, 1955, pp. 39–40.

144 Allan Mitchell, '"A Situation of Inferiority". French military reorganization after the defeat of 1870', *American Historical Review*, 86/1, 1981, pp. 49–62.

145 Jean-Charles Jauffret, 'Armée et pouvoir politique. La question des troupes spéciales chargés du maintien de l'ordre en France de 1871 à 1914', *Revue historique*, 270, 1983, pp. 98–144.

146 Jean Rabaut, *L'Antimilitarisme en France, 1870–1975*, Hachette, 1975.

147 William H. Schneider, *An Empire for the Masses. The French Popular Image of Africa, 1870–1900*, Greenwood Press, 1982.

148 Jean Baubérot, 'L'Antiprotestantisme politique à la fin du XIXe siècle', *Revue d'Histoire et de Philosophie des Religions*, 52, 1972, pp. 449–84; 53, 1973, pp. 177–221.

149 Zeev Sternhell, *Maurice Barrès et le Nationalisme français*, Armand Colin, 1972.

150 Raoul Girardet, *Le Nationalisme français, 1871–1914*, Armand Colin, 1966.

151 Eugen Weber, *The Nationalist Revival in France, 1905–1914*, University of California Press, 1959.

152 Eric Cahm, *Péguy et le Nationalisme français*, Cahiers de l'Amitié Charles Péguy, 1972.

153 Dan P. Silverman, *Reluctant Union. Alsace-Lorraine and Imperial Germany, 1871–1918*, Pennsylvania State University, 1972.

154 John F. Keiger, *France and the Origins of the First World War*, Macmillan, 1983.

155 Gordon Wright, *Poincaré and the French Presidency*, Stanford University Press, 1942.

156 Jacques Julliard, 'La C.G.T. devant la guerre, 1900–1914', *Le Mouvement Social*, 49, 1964, pp. 47–62.

157 Jean-Jacques Fiechter, *Le Socialisme français de l'Affaire Dreyfus à la Grande Guerre*, Droz, 1965.

158 Georges Haupt, *Socialism and the Great War*, Oxford University Press, 1972.

159 Jean-Jacques Becker, *The Great War and the French People*, Berg, 1985.

THE THIRD REPUBLIC ASSESSED

160 Laurence Wylie, *Village in the Vaucluse*, Harvard University Press, 1957.

161 François Caron, *An Economic History of Modern France*, Methuen, 1979.

162 Marc Ferro, *The Great War, 1914–1918*, Routledge and Kegan Paul, 1973.

Index